THROUGH THE FIRE

A Victim's Guide

JOSHUA BARRETT

i

Dedication

To Mindy Cunningham, whose encouragement gave me the final push I needed to bring my words to life. Her belief in me and her inspiration motivated me to share my story with the world, and for that, I am deeply grateful.

Contents

Author's Note

Life challenges each of us in ways that often feel overwhelming. We all face personal battles that weigh us down, yet each of us deserves a genuine chance to pursue a life of peace, joy, and fulfillment—a life free from the burdens of our past.

For many years, I sought an easy path to happiness. I tried countless forms of avoidance, only to come to an essential truth: the only way forward is through direct confrontation with our struggles.

In time, I took the first real step toward reclaiming my life. I made the deliberate choice to free myself from addiction and release past pain and shame. This journey wasn't easy; it demanded a conscious decision to place my well-being above all else.

I soon realized that if we are blessed enough to make it out of the fire, we are obligated to reach back in. After finding success in recovery, I began to lose friends at an alarming rate—friends who had also sought recovery or mental health stability but succumbed to overdose or suicide. In my first few years of sobriety alone, I lost over 100 friends. The pandemic intensified these tragedies, pushing me to seek a deeper understanding of why so many couldn't find a way through and how I might offer an approach for those who feel disconnected from typical self-help guidance.

In this book, I have shared the insights and practices that helped me achieve a sense of peace and recovery. I've taken care to present these ideas clearly and practically, with the hope that they may integrate into your daily life and lead you toward healing.

This path isn't easy, and it requires a solid commitment. To transform your life, you must decide that you are willing to do the necessary work. I encourage you to pause, consider this commitment deeply, and make the choice to pursue the freedom you deserve.

Chapter One:
Introduction To Joshua's Journey

We all carry scars from life's hardships, some deeper than others. Trauma, in its countless forms, can leave a permanent mark on our souls, shaping how we view the world and interact with those around us. For many of us who have experienced trauma, the concept of a "normal life" becomes both a distant dream and an urgent necessity.

I remember countless nights lying awake, yearning for the simplicity of normalcy. While others dreamed of fame or fortune, my deepest desire was far more fundamental – to function, to exist without the constant shadow of my past looming over me. This longing became a driving force in my journey of recovery, a beacon of hope in the darkness of my struggles.

For years, I lived as a prisoner of my trauma, viewing every interaction and opportunity through the lens of victimhood. Trust became a foreign concept, and love felt like a luxury I couldn't afford.

I built walls to protect myself, never realizing they were also keeping me isolated from the very connections that could help me heal.

Life became a series of cycles – periods of apparent stability followed by devastating collapses. No matter how convincingly I told myself and others that I was "fine," the wounded part of me would eventually resurface, tearing down whatever progress I had made since the last breakdown.

Through conversations with fellow survivors, I discovered a universal truth: the path of recovery is rarely linear. We all experience moments of strength and clarity punctuated by periods of struggle. The key difference lies not in the absence of pain but in how we choose to confront and integrate it into our lives.

As Buddha wisely said, "Holding on to anger is like grasping a hot coal with the intent of throwing it at someone else; you are the one who gets burned." The same can be said for holding onto our trauma. To truly heal, we must find the courage to face our pain head-on and examine it with compassion and understanding.

This process isn't about erasing the past or pretending it didn't happen. Instead, it's about reclaiming control over our lives and refusing to let our traumas define us. The "victim" within us may always be present, but it doesn't have to be in the driver's seat.

Achieving that longed-for "normal life" isn't about reaching a fixed destination. It's an ongoing journey of self-discovery, forgiveness, and growth.

As someone who has walked this path, I understand the challenges and setbacks that come with healing from trauma. There were times when the journey felt impossible, when the weight of the past seemed too heavy to bear. But I'm here to tell you that change is possible. With patience, perseverance, and the right support, we can learn to live life on our own terms.

Remember, your trauma may be a part of your story, but it doesn't have to be the whole story. You have the power to write new chapters to fill your life with joy, connection, and purpose. The road may not always be easy, but I promise you, it's worth every step.

This journey, a labyrinth of despair and hope, has been a relentless teacher. In the chapters that follow, we will delve into the heart of darkness, exploring the concepts of forgiveness and acceptance. Through personal reflections, research-backed insights, and the wisdom of others, we will illuminate a path toward healing and growth. Your journey to healing and normalcy has already begun – now, let's take the next steps together.

Together, we will learn to transform shadows into stepping stones.

As I reflect on my life's journey, I'm struck by the profound impact of early trauma and the long, winding road to recovery. My story begins with abandonment - my birth mother leaving when I was born, setting the stage for a childhood marked by instability and abuse.

Growing up with my biological father was a nightmare of abuse, not just for me but for many children around me. His eventual imprisonment after a drunk driving accident was both a relief and another upheaval in my young life. The cycle continued with my aunt and uncle, who, unprepared for the responsibility, placed me in foster care.

By the time I was adopted, I had been diagnosed as psychotic and spent years in mental health facilities. Just as I thought I might find stability, my adoptive parents divorced as I entered high school. Yet, somehow, I managed to navigate those teenage years with a semblance of normalcy, free from the anxiety and PTSD symptoms that would later define my life.

It wasn't until I moved to New York for college and work as a youth pastor that the floodgates opened. Suddenly, I was drowning in flashbacks, the past I had so carefully buried rushing to the surface. When these mental struggles manifested as physical seizures, I returned home to Indiana, scared and confused.

Then came the turning point that would shape the next two decades of my life. At a graduation party, I drank alcohol for the first time in years and experienced a moment of clarity - or so I thought. The anxiety, the flashbacks, the fear - they all disappeared, if only temporarily. Instead of seeking professional help, I chose the path of least resistance, using substances to numb the pain and function in society.

For almost 20 years, I lived in cycles. I'd achieve success, only to watch it crumble as my substance use spiraled out of control. I'd lose jobs, embarrass myself, and simply move on, starting fresh in a new place with new people. College became a distant memory as I found myself living in my car, a far cry from the future I had once envisioned.

Relationships suffered, too. I kept people at arm's length, living a life built on lies and half-truths. The reality of my childhood remained unspoken, a heavy secret I carried alone. When the facade inevitably cracked, I'd simply disappear, leaving behind the wreckage of friendships and start anew elsewhere.

Financial struggles became a constant companion. The need for more substances to stay numb led me down darker paths - lying, cheating, stealing. I was anxious angry, taking everything personally and lashing out at those around me.

Looking back, I realize now that I was caught in a vicious cycle of trauma and addiction. Each attempt to escape my past only deepened the hole I was digging for myself. Yet, even in my darkest moments, a small part of me held onto hope - hope that one day, I could break free from this pattern and truly heal.

It all began with loneliness. But more than that, it was a moment of true hopelessness. I had tried everything I thought would work, and nothing had. I stood at the edge, feeling like this was it - this was who I was destined to be, how I was fated to live. My resources were depleted, and my options were exhausted.

Just when I thought all was lost, a memory from my youth group surfaced - a verse about a way being provided when there seemed to be none. In that instant, something shifted. I went from utter despair to a tiny flicker of hope.

I'd lost so much - my kids, my wife, my sense of self. Part of me felt I deserved this fate. My childhood had left me feeling worthless, and as an adult, I'd made choices that only reinforced that belief. I'd become an addict, a drunk, a liar, and a thief. When I looked in the mirror, all I saw was a monster undeserving of a place in society.

But in that rock-bottom moment of brokenness, that glimmer of hope pierced through. I didn't know what the solution would be, but I clung to that spark with everything I had. It was enough to keep me going, enough to make me think that maybe, just maybe, there was a way forward.

By morning, I found the strength to try again. I could go to a meeting, maybe even give church another shot. I didn't know if everything would be okay, but I had just enough hope to keep me from giving up entirely.

That night of prayer and meditation, filled with tears and soul-searching, gave me the courage to face another day. It led me to a meeting, which inspired me to go to church, which strengthened my faith enough to return to another meeting, where I connected with a sponsor. One small step led to another, and another, over the course of years.

Now, when I share my story with those I sponsor, I emphasize this point: I had no idea what the solution would be in that moment of despair. My hope came from somewhere beyond myself, a tiny lifeline in a sea of darkness. I held onto it with all my might, and it carried me through.

This journey has taught me that even in our darkest moments, hope can find us. It may be small, it may be fragile, but it's there. And if we're brave enough to grasp it, to nurture it, it can lead us out of the depths and into a life we never thought possible.

Each step of my recovery built on the last, creating a path I could never have imagined in those hopeless moments. Today, I stand as living proof that change is possible, that redemption is real, and that no matter how far we've fallen, we can always find our way back to the light.

It took 20 years, but I finally found the courage to face my demons sober. The road to recovery has been challenging, but it's also been incredibly rewarding. I've learned to speak my truth to confront the pain of my past instead of running from it. I've discovered the strength that was within me all along - the strength that helped me survive those early years of abuse and instability.

To anyone out there struggling with similar demons, I want you to know that it's never too late to change your story. The path to healing isn't easy, but it's worth every step. Embrace honesty - with yourself and others. Seek support - you don't have to face this alone. Practice self-compassion - your past doesn't define you.

Remember, the very fact that you've survived this far is a testament to your resilience. You have the power to transform your pain into strength and your struggles into wisdom. It won't happen overnight, but with each small step, you're moving toward a life of authenticity, connection, and purpose.

Your journey of healing and self-discovery has already begun. Trust in the process, believe in yourself, and know that a brighter future awaits. You've carried the weight of your past for so long - now it's time to lighten that load and embrace the possibilities that lie ahead.

It's essential to remember that healing is a personal odyssey. There is no one-size-fits-all approach to mending the wounds of trauma. Yet, within the shared experiences of countless survivors, we find a common thread: the unwavering human spirit's capacity for resilience and transformation.

In the chapters to come, we will delve deeper into the complexities of forgiveness and acceptance, exploring how these concepts can serve as powerful tools for healing. We will examine the science behind trauma and the brain, unraveling the intricate ways it shapes our thoughts, emotions, and behaviors. Through personal stories and expert insights, we will illuminate pathways to recovery, offering practical strategies and coping mechanisms.

Remember, this book is not merely a collection of information; it's an invitation to a profound exploration of your own inner landscape. It's a space where you can find solace, understanding, and inspiration as you navigate the intricate tapestry of your experiences.

As we journey together, let us hold onto the hope that emerges from the depths of despair. Let us embrace the power of vulnerability, recognizing that it is through sharing our stories that we create a stronger, more compassionate world. And let us cultivate a spirit of gratitude, finding beauty and meaning even in the midst of life's challenges.

Together, we will transform shadows into stepping stones, writing a narrative of hope, resilience, and triumph.

∾

Chapter Two:
The Power Of Acceptance

"The first step toward change is awareness.
The second step is acceptance."

–Nathaniel Branden

Acceptance is one of those words that is frequently employed, but when you really dig into it, you realize it's not as simple as it sounds. So, acceptance isn't about letting the problem linger indefinitely; it's about acknowledging its presence and figuring out what to do next.

When we talk about acceptance, especially in the context of personal growth, we are talking about something deeply personal and, let's be honest, often really tough. It is not about throwing in the towel or saying, "Well, that's just how things are, and there is nothing I can do about it." It is way far from it. Acceptance is about looking at a situation square in the eye and saying, "Okay, this is what happened. Now what?"

The First Step: Calling It What It Is

I once heard someone say, "Say it out loud, and it will take its power away." And you know what? They were right. There is something almost magical about hearing the words you have kept bottled up inside. The words might be scary, uncomfortable, or even shameful, but saying them out loud makes them real and, in a strange way, manageable.

For a long time, I tried to pretend that the abuse I experienced as a child didn't happen. I buried it deep, convinced that if I ignored it long enough, it would just disappear. But trauma doesn't just go away because you want it to. When you keep ignoring a pebble in your shoe, you can limp along for a while, but eventually, it is going to start digging into your foot, and you will have no choice but to stop and deal with it.

For me, that moment came when I finally admitted to myself, "Yes, I was abused." It wasn't easy. In fact, it felt like tearing open an old wound. But the moment I said it out loud, something shifted. The power that those unspoken words had over me started to fade. I wasn't "approving" of what happened, nor was I saying it was okay. I was simply calling it what it was. And that was the first step toward healing.

Radical Acceptance: Meeting Life Where It Is

Now, let's talk about something called radical acceptance. It sounds a bit intense, but really, it's just a fancy way of saying that we need to acknowledge reality as it is without getting caught up in what we wish it were. We must be present and honest with ourselves. If something is sad, say it is sad. If something is frustrating, say it is frustrating. Take a deep breath and say, "Okay, this is how I feel right now." No judgment, no denial, just honesty.

Radical acceptance isn't about sitting in your emotions and letting them take over. That would be like getting stuck in quicksand. You recognize the emotion, give it a nod, and then move on. This is how you can acknowledge what is so you can figure out what to do next. It is kind of like navigating a map. You can't plot a course to where you want to go if you don't know where you are starting from.

Acceptance is a powerful tool in healing, especially for trauma victims. It's not about surrendering or giving up but rather acknowledging the reality of our experiences and choosing to engage with them in a way that promotes growth and well-being.[1] Imagine you are carrying a heavy backpack filled with rocks. Each rock represents a painful memory, a trauma, or an emotion you'd rather not deal with. Now, you have two options: you can either continue to carry this burden, pretending it doesn't exist, or you can take a moment to sit down, open the backpack, and start taking out the rocks one by one. Acceptance is that moment of sitting down, recognizing the weight you are carrying, and deciding to do something about it.

For trauma survivors, acceptance can seem daunting. After all, why would anyone want to accept something as painful as trauma? But the twist is accepting your trauma doesn't mean you agree with it or that it was justified. It simply means acknowledging its impact on

---

[1] Ford, R. (2022). *Creating Safe Spaces: The Power of Trauma-Informed Language*. Reggie Ford. Retrieved from https://reggiedford.com

your life without letting it define you. By accepting your experiences, you give yourself permission to feel, process, and ultimately heal.[2]

One way to approach acceptance is through the concept of self-compassion. This involves treating yourself with the same kindness and understanding you would offer to a friend. Trauma often leaves us feeling unworthy or broken, but self-compassion challenges this narrative by reminding us that we are deserving of love and care, even in our darkest moments. This helps us recognize that suffering is a part of life, but it doesn't have to be the whole story.[3]

In practice, self-compassion might look like giving yourself a break when you are overwhelmed or allowing yourself to feel sad without judgment. You let yourself be gentle with you as you navigate the ups and downs of healing. Remember, healing isn't linear, and there is no right or wrong way to do it. What matters is that you are taking steps, however small, toward accepting your reality and moving forward.[2]

Another key aspect of acceptance is cognitive defusion, a technique used in Acceptance and Commitment Therapy (ACT). Cognitive defusion helps us to distance ourselves from our thoughts and emotions, allowing us to observe them without becoming overwhelmed.[4] For instance, if you are haunted by a traumatic memory, instead of trying to push it away, cognitive defusion encourages you to acknowledge the memory without letting it control

---

[2] Germer, C. (2018). *The Mindful Path to Self-Compassion*. CPTSD Foundation. Retrieved from https://cptsdfoundation.org
[3] Neff, K. (2022). *Self-Compassion and Childhood Trauma Recovery*. CPTSD Foundation. Retrieved from https://cptsdfoundation.org

[4] GoodTherapy. (2017). *How Acceptance and Commitment Therapy Helps with Posttraumatic Stress*. GoodTherapy. Retrieved from https://www.goodtherapy.org

you. You watch the clouds pass by in the sky—acknowledge them, but don't chase them.

Radical acceptance, another powerful tool, teaches us to embrace reality as it is, not as we wish it to be. You don't need to give up on change or improvement; rather, recognize the present moment for what it is. [4] By accepting the things we cannot change, we free up the mental and emotional energy to focus on what we can do to create a better future. Being in a storm, you decide to stop fighting the wind—by accepting it, you find a way to navigate through it more effectively.

For those who have experienced trauma, acceptance might involve acknowledging the pain without letting it dictate your future. You understand that while trauma is a part of your story, it doesn't have to be the whole book. [1] Acceptance allows you to reclaim your narrative, integrating the past with the present and moving toward a future where you are in control.

This practice of radical acceptance has been life-changing for me. I used to hold onto so much pain and shame that I was constantly overwhelmed. My mind was like a dark storm, full of chaotic thoughts that only created more pain. I tried to numb it with substance abuse, thinking that if I could just avoid feeling, I'd be okay. But avoidance is like putting a bandage on a deep cut without cleaning it first. The wound just festers.

It wasn't until I started practicing radical acceptance—acknowledging the pain, the shame, the fear—that things began to change. I started small, understanding that this was my reality and that there had to be a way through it. It wasn't easy, but it was necessary.

Speaking The Unspoken: The Weight Of Words

There was a pivotal moment in my journey where I had to confront everything I had been holding onto. I had an old sponsor who suggested I write down everything—the darkest memories, the deepest shame—and then read them out loud to him. Just the thought of it terrified me. I rescheduled our meeting four times because I was so afraid of what he might think of me if he knew everything.

But eventually, I mustered up the courage to do it. I remember sitting there, reading those words, and feeling the weight of each one. It was like carrying a heavy backpack for years and suddenly dropping it to the ground. When I was done, my sponsor looked at me and said, "I love you, man." And that was it. I cried, not out of sadness, but out of relief.

After that, something amazing happened. As I walked to my car, I noticed that my body felt different. My cheeks were no longer tight, my shoulders weren't hunched, and I felt lighter—physically and emotionally. For years, I had been carrying all this tension, not realizing how it was affecting me. But once I spoke those words, it was as if my body finally exhaled. The headaches, the stomach aches, the back pain—all of it started to fade.

Thus, remember, acceptance isn't just about emotional healing; it's about physical healing, too. Our bodies carry the stress of unresolved trauma, and when we let go of that trauma, our bodies can finally start to relax.

You might be wondering, "Why is acceptance so important? Can't I just move on without it?" Well, acceptance is the foundation of everything else. Without it, you are building your house on sand.

Acceptance gives you the stability you need to start healing and start building a life that isn't defined by your past.

When you accept what happened—whether it is a trauma, a mistake, or a difficult situation—you are not giving up. You are simply acknowledging that this is your starting point and that you have been dealt a certain number of cards. You might not like the cards you have been given, but you can't play the game until you accept what is in your hand.

And once you do, everything changes. Your anxiety starts to decrease because you are no longer fighting against reality. Your confidence grows because you are not hiding from the truth anymore. You start to see people and situations more clearly because you are not viewing them through the lens of unprocessed pain.

For example, for years, I struggled with trust issues because my mother left when I was born. I was always convinced that everyone in my life would eventually leave me, too. But when I finally accepted that my mom's actions were her own and they didn't mean everyone else would do the same, I was able to build real relationships. Acceptance helped me to trust again, and that trust has been the foundation for every meaningful connection I have made since.

Health Risks Of Not Practicing Acceptance

Ignoring unresolved trauma and refusing to accept past events can lead to significant physical health issues. Chronic stress from unresolved emotional pain can elevate blood pressure, leading to hypertension, which increases the risk of heart disease.[5]

Chronic stress also affects the brain, impairing memory and increasing the risk of mental health disorders like depression and anxiety. [6]

Additionally, prolonged stress can weaken the immune system, making the body more susceptible to infections and illnesses. [7]

Over time, this can shorten lifespan, highlighting the importance of acceptance not just for emotional well-being but for physical health and longevity.

The Daily Practice Of Acceptance

The truth is acceptance isn't a one-time thing. It is a daily practice, like brushing your teeth or making your bed. This is something you have to work at, especially if you are carrying a lot of baggage from the past. But the good news is, the more you practice it, the easier it gets.

One of the most effective ways to practice acceptance is through journaling. Every day, set aside a few minutes to reflect on what happened that day. Write down any moments that stand out—whether they were positive or negative—and be honest with yourself

---

[5] American Heart Association. (2016). *Stress and Heart Health.* https://www.heart.org/en/healthy-living/healthy-lifestyle/stress-management/stress-and-heart-health

[6] Harvard Health Publishing. (2020). *Stress can have lasting effects on your brain.* https://www.health.harvard.edu/staying-healthy/stress-and-the-brain

[7] Mayo Clinic. (2022). *Stress symptoms: Effects on your body and behavior.* https://www.mayoclinic.org/healthy-lifestyle/stress-management/in-depth/stress-symptoms/art-20050987

about how you felt. If something makes you angry or sad, acknowledge it. Don't try to sugarcoat it or push it away. Just write it down and let it be.

Meditation is another powerful tool for practicing acceptance. Even just five minutes a day can make a difference. The goal of meditation isn't to clear your mind completely but to sit with whatever thoughts and feelings come up without judgment. This is to acknowledge what is there without getting attached to it. Sometimes, all we need is a moment of stillness to really understand what we are feeling and why.

If there is a person in your life that you need to confront—whether it's someone who hurt you or someone you have hurt yourself—that will be covered in a later chapter on forgiveness. But for now, focus on accepting what is rather than what you wish it were.

The beautiful thing about acceptance is that it doesn't just apply to the big, painful experiences in life. It works in every area of your life. Once you get the hang of it, you will find that acceptance can help you navigate all sorts of challenges, from the mundane to the monumental.

For example, I used to get incredibly frustrated with traffic. It would drive me up the wall, especially when I was running late. But once I started practicing acceptance, I realized that getting angry wasn't going to make the cars move any faster. So, instead of stewing in my frustration, I started using that time to practice patience. I'd listen to a podcast or just take a few deep breaths and remind myself that this, too, shall pass. Over time, traffic became less of an annoyance and more of an opportunity to practice staying calm.

The same goes for interactions with others. Acceptance gives you patience, not just with yourself, but with everyone around you. When you accept that people are who they are—flaws and all—you stop expecting them to be perfect. You stop taking things personally and start seeing things more clearly. This doesn't mean you let people walk all over you, but it does mean you approach situations with more understanding and less frustration.

In my own life, acceptance has been the key to building a strong, healthy relationship with my wife. For years, I kept things bottled up, afraid to share my true feelings and experiences with her. But once I started practicing acceptance—of myself and of her—I found that we could be more open with each other. Our relationship grew stronger because we were both able to be our true selves without fear of judgment.

The impact this has had on my relationship with my kids has been incredible. I used to be so wrapped up in my own anxiety and fear that I couldn't fully enjoy the time I spent with them. But now, I am able to let loose, have fun, and really connect with them in a way I never could before.

The Rewards Of Acceptance

The rewards of acceptance are immense. When you practice it daily, it becomes a part of who you are. You start to move through the world with more ease, more grace, and a lot less stress. Little frustrations—like traffic or long lines—don't phase you anymore. You stop seeing the world as a place full of obstacles and start seeing it as a place full of opportunities.

Yet, the best part is when you are not weighed down by the past, you are free to just be. You can live in the moment, experience life as it comes, and enjoy the little things without worrying about what might go wrong. Acceptance doesn't mean you stop caring; it means you stop letting fear and anxiety control your life.

Every morning, I have a routine that helps me maintain this process. I journal, I meditate, I study something that inspires me, and I take time to reflect on everything I am grateful for. These practices keep me grounded, help me stay in the moment, and remind me of all the blessings in my life.

So, as you move forward on your own journey, I encourage you to embrace acceptance as a daily practice. Start small, be patient with yourself, and remember that it is okay if it takes time. The path to acceptance is a journey, not a destination. But the more you practice, the more you will find that it's not just possible—it's life-changing.

In the end, acceptance isn't just about dealing with the tough stuff but opening yourself up to all the good things life has to offer, too. Because when you stop fighting against what is, you make room for what could be. And that is where the real magic happens.

Chapter Three:
Understanding And Practicing Forgiveness

*"To forgive is to set a prisoner free
and discover that the prisoner was you."*

– Lewis B. Smedes

Forgiveness isn't about letting someone off the hook or pretending that what they did was okay. It's all about you and your well-being. We often think that we need some sort of justice or payback to move on. If you've ever felt that way, you're not alone. It's a natural instinct, but it's one that can seriously mess with your peace of mind.

When you view forgiveness as a transaction— "They hurt me, so they need to make it right before I forgive them"—you set yourself up for a never-ending cycle of pain. The constant focus on getting that apology keeps you stuck in anger and frustration, and let's be honest, it only makes you more miserable.

Here's the thing: forgiveness is about you taking control. It's saying, "Yeah, that happened, but I'm not letting it ruin my day today." It's about moving on so that you're not dragging the weight of that hurt around with you, letting it spill over into other areas of your life.

Forgiveness: The Ultimate Power Move

Forgiveness is just like acceptance in action. It's about letting go of the pain that's tied to someone or something and starting to write a new story where you're in charge. Think of it as hitting the reset button—you're not forgetting what happened, but you're choosing not to let it control you anymore.

At its core, forgiveness is a conscious decision to release that resentment or anger. It's saying, "They did me wrong; it hurt, but I'm not going to let it keep hurting me." When you forgive, you're not letting anyone off the hook; you're just freeing yourself from the burden of carrying that hurt around.

So, if you're still holding onto something, maybe it's time to try a little forgiveness, not for them, but for you. After all, it's your peace of mind on the line.

For a long time, my life was ruled by my inability to accept and forgive. The hurt I experienced as a child stayed with me, affecting every relationship I had. Every day, I relived that pain, and with each passing day, my anger grew. That anger became my excuse for everything—whether it was drinking, using substances, or just being mean and impatient. I played the victim card hard, convincing myself that my pain justified my actions.

This mindset made it nearly impossible to maintain any meaningful relationships. I'd end friendships and business partnerships over the smallest issues because I was carrying around the unresolved pain and unforgiveness from my past. Instead of giving people a fair shot, I let my old wounds poison every new interaction. It was like everyone I met had to answer for the wrongs others had done to me.

Looking back, I realize that I let pain, fear, and anger control not only my actions but also how I treated people. No one ever got a fair shake from me because I was dragging decades of baggage into every situation. My life became a lonely, angry mess because I couldn't trust anyone enough to form real relationships.

When I finally started practicing acceptance, I was shocked at how much of my pain had nothing to do with what was happening today. My obsession with getting justice only left me feeling angry and disappointed all the time. But with acceptance, I began to see things differently. I made a list of people I needed to forgive—some I'd never see again and others who would never apologize. But I realized that forgiving them was about freeing myself, not about getting an apology.

Forgiveness doesn't have to be a grand gesture. You don't have to face the person and say, "I forgive you." This isn't about them; it's about you. For me, I found that writing letters was helpful, but what really worked was talking to my phone in selfie mode, pretending it was the person I needed to forgive. I'd say everything I needed to say—sometimes yelling, sometimes crying—and with each video, I felt lighter. Once I was done, I deleted the videos and moved on.

Some things come back, and that's okay. I've had to forgive the same person or situation more than once. When old feelings creep up,

I still use my video journal method to let them out. It's an ongoing process, but each time, I feel a bit more at peace.

The hardest part of all this was learning to forgive myself. As an addict, I hurt a lot of people. I wasn't the dad I wanted to be, and I was a lousy husband before I got sober. The guilt and shame I felt were suffocating, and just like unresolved anger toward others, they poisoned my relationships. That shame kept me trapped in a cycle of self-loathing, where every mistake I made reinforced the belief that I wasn't good enough.

But here's the thing: when we forgive ourselves, just like when we forgive others, we start to break that cycle. We change the stories we tell ourselves and begin to see new possibilities. It's not easy, and it doesn't happen overnight, but each time we forgive—whether it's someone else or ourselves—we take another step toward living a life that's not controlled by the past.

So if you're holding onto something, whether it's anger toward someone else or guilt toward yourself, maybe it's time to let it go. Not for them, but for you. Because, in the end, you deserve to live without the weight of yesterday's pain.

The Science Behind Forgiveness

Forgiveness isn't just a feel-good idea; it's got some serious science backing it up. According to research from Johns Hopkins Medicine, practicing forgiveness can lead to lower blood pressure, reduced anxiety, and even better heart health.[8] Harvard Health also notes that

---

[8] Johns Hopkins Medicine. (n.d.). Forgiveness: Your health depends on it. https://www.hopkinsmedicine.org/health/wellness-and-prevention/forgiveness-your-health-depends-on-it

forgiveness is linked to fewer symptoms of depression and a stronger immune system.[9] So, if you're looking for a way to improve both your mental and physical well-being, forgiveness is a solid choice.

Steps to Cultivate Forgiveness

First things first—let's talk acceptance. Often, the things that haunt us are buried so deep in our minds that we don't even realize they're affecting us. But before you can forgive, you've got to acknowledge what's causing the pain. Remember that list I mentioned in the acceptance chapter? Pull that out because it's time to start addressing each item.

Here's the plan: write down, video yourself, or say out loud everything you need to express to the person who hurt you. Don't hold back—let it all out, whether you're venting, shouting, or crying. This might sound intense, but it helps to release the pent-up emotions and put the situation into perspective.

After you've unloaded, take a moment to acknowledge the pain and its ongoing impact on your life. This step is crucial—it's like shining a light on a wound so it can finally start to heal. Then, make a conscious decision about your future. Say things like, "What you did was wrong, but I'm not letting it control me anymore," or "You've had enough power over my life; it's time for me to take it back." These mantras can be your go-to whenever those old pains try to sneak back in. Remember, this is a process—think of it as a marathon, not a sprint.

---

[9] Harvard Health Publishing. (2022). The power of forgiveness: Why letting go of grudges is good for your health. https://www.health.harvard.edu/mind-and-mood/the-power-of-forgiveness

According to the American Psychological Association (APA), forgiveness can be a long journey, but it's one worth taking. By processing your feelings and letting go of unrealistic expectations, you're setting the stage for a life free from past burdens.[10] Confirmation bias tells us that we'll experience what we focus on, so choose to focus on healing and peace. You've got the keys to your own recovery—now it's time to use them.

Forgiving Others Vs. Forgiving Yourself

Now, let's talk about the difference between forgiving others and forgiving yourself. If you've ever felt like you're your own worst critic, you're not alone. It's often easier to see the good in others than in ourselves. And that's pretty logical when you think about it—no one knows all our flaws and mistakes like we do. We're the ones who remember every lie, every misstep, and every regret.

This is where the victim mindset comes in. When we mess up, it's easy to fall into the trap of thinking, "I always get it wrong," or "There's something fundamentally wrong with me." That's just confirmation bias working against you, reinforcing a negative narrative.

In my own experience, forgiving others came much easier than forgiving myself. But here's the twist: it was through forgiving others that I finally learned to cut myself some slack. When I managed to forgive my birth father for the abuse and my birth mother for the abandonment, I realized that if they deserved forgiveness, maybe I did too.

---

[10] American Psychological Association. (n.d.). Forgiveness: Letting go of grudges and bitterness. https://www.apa.org/topics/forgiveness

So, if you're struggling with self-forgiveness, start by extending that grace to others. It might just make it a little easier to see that you're worthy of forgiveness as well.

The Challenge Of Forgiveness

Forgiveness isn't always a walk in the park. Let's face it—when someone hurts you, that pain is real, and your feelings are completely valid. The tricky part is figuring out how to honor your experience while also not letting it drag you down day after day.

When we get hurt, there's this natural urge to feel whole again. We often think that means someone has to fix things—if only they'd apologize or make it right. But here's the kicker: even if they do say sorry, you'll still have to deal with your own pain. Remember, forgiveness is all about you, not them. So, whether they're remorseful or not is pretty irrelevant to your healing.

Another common misconception? Some folks think that forgiving means forgetting. If you find yourself saying, "I can't forgive until I forget," that's just another trap. Our brains are wired to remember things that hurt us. It's like having an alarm system for pain! So, while you might not be able to erase those memories, you can definitely heal so that they don't keep you stuck in a loop of hurt.

And just because you forgive someone doesn't mean you have to jump back into the same relationship you had before. You can forgive and still keep your distance. Setting boundaries is key here! If we just forgave and forgot, we'd likely find ourselves facing the same issues over and over again. Think of forgiveness as a way to say, "I forgive you so I can move on," while also protecting yourself from getting hurt again.

Sometimes, people expect you to forgive them and then act like nothing ever happened. That's not how forgiveness works! It's not about wiping the slate clean; it's about letting go of the pain. You forgive for your own peace of mind, so you don't have to carry that hurt around.

Practical Tips For Fostering Forgiveness

Now that we've tackled some of the hurdles to forgiveness. Let's explore some practical exercises and tips to help you along the way.

1. Empathy is Your Friend

One great tool I like to use is the "2 x 4 rule." I picked this up years ago in a recovery meeting. The "2x4 rule" is a cognitive reframing technique often utilized in recovery programs and personal development contexts. This principle encourages individuals to shift their perspective when interpreting others' actions. The rule is simple: they didn't do it for you but for them. This mindset shift can really help you find forgiveness, even for deep hurts and everyday frustrations.

Picture this: someone cuts you off in traffic. It's easy to feel like a victim and get all riled up. But guess what? That driver probably didn't wake up thinking, "Today, I'll annoy someone by cutting them off!" They might have missed a turn or just been in a rush. When you shift your perspective to recognize that they're just trying to get to their destination, it's easier to forgive at the moment. After all, we all make mistakes, and don't we hope for a little grace when we do?

2. Journaling for Clarity

Writing can be incredibly therapeutic. Journaling your feelings or even creating a video journal can help you process what happened and how it affected you. It's like having a heart-to-heart with yourself, and it's a great way to reflect on your emotions.

3. Role Play for Real Life

If you're comfortable, try role-playing with a trusted friend or a professional. This can be an effective way to explore your feelings and work through the process of forgiveness. Talking it out can help you see things from different angles and find your way to a more forgiving mindset.

Forgiveness can be one of the toughest challenges we face, but it's also one of the most rewarding. We take back control over our lives by shifting our focus from seeking justice to reclaiming our own peace. Remember, forgiving someone—or yourself—isn't about forgetting or pretending nothing happened. It's about freeing yourself from the chains of past hurts so you can live more fully in the present. The process might be ongoing, with setbacks and struggles, but each step you take toward forgiveness lightens your load and brings you closer to true peace of mind. Keep practicing, keep moving forward, and give yourself the grace you deserve.

Chapter Four:
Overcoming Trauma

"It is not the load that breaks you down; it's the way you carry it."

– Lou Holtz

Trauma, hardship, and challenges often seem overwhelming, as if they weigh heavily on the mind and heart. Yet, it is not always the weight of the trauma itself that leads to exhaustion. More often, the way we choose to carry that emotional load determines whether it becomes unbearable or manageable.

We often think of trauma as some huge, devastating event – and sometimes it is. But trauma can also be more subtle. At its core, trauma is anything that changes the way we experience the world, any experience that leaves a scar on our perception. For some, it's a life-altering event like a car accident; for others, it's something as insidious as the quiet loss of trust after a betrayal. Trauma is personal, and because everyone's experiences are unique, it can be hard for others to understand exactly why you feel the way you do. That's one of the biggest challenges with trauma – it can feel like you are alone, cursed to live in a constant loop of pain that no one else understands.

Regrettably, trauma seeps into everything. It creeps into your self-image, your relationships, and even your day-to-day decisions. It makes you question everything, and not in a good way. The worst part is you question it all through the lens of that traumatic experience. It's like looking at life through a pair of broken glasses – the cracks warp your vision, but you still try to navigate the world as if nothing's wrong. And before you know it, you are stuck in a loop where every flat tire, every bad day, feels like the universe is conspiring against you.

This is where trauma can get overwhelming. Suddenly, everything feels like it's out to get you. It's not just paranoia – it's your brain's natural response to unresolved trauma.[11] Your brain is wired to protect you, and if it thinks danger is lurking around every corner, it will go into overdrive, scanning the world for threats. This heightened state of fear often leads to panic, trust issues, and even a belief that you're always the victim.

I know this all too well.

I grew up in a childhood filled with abuse in every form you can imagine, combined with a deep sense of abandonment from birth, which left me with emotional scars that ran deep. Those early experiences shaped how I saw the world – and myself. I felt like I had no worth, like no one could ever truly love or care for me. On top of what I went through, I also saw other kids around me being hurt, and

---

[11] NCBI. (2019). *The effects of trauma on the brain*. National Center for Biotechnology Information. https://www.ncbi.nlm.nih.gov

there was nothing I could do. I was too young, too powerless. That feeling of helplessness haunted me well into adulthood.

The foster care system only made things worse. Moving from house to house just solidified the belief that no one could ever truly love me. Each move felt like a confirmation of my worthlessness. By the time I was adopted, I had severe mental health issues that led to frequent hospitalizations. In and out of institutions, It felt like I could never find stable ground. By the time I reached any semblance of stability, the damage had already been done. My self-worth was non-existent, and I was paralyzed by a fear of failure.

That fear kept me from doing anything. I was so afraid that trying and failing would only prove what I already believed – that I was worthless. So, I didn't try. I achieved very little, and when I did achieve something, my fear of losing it all would inevitably lead me to lose it. Self-sabotage became my go-to move. I'd destroy anything good in my life before it had a chance to leave me.

Trauma affects not just your emotions but your brain as well. Studies from the National Center for Biotechnology Information (NCBI) show that trauma can cause lasting changes in the brain's structure and function, particularly in areas related to fear and stress (NCBI, 2019). The amygdala, the part of the brain responsible for processing fear, goes into overdrive, while the prefrontal cortex – the part that helps you reason and make decisions – can struggle to keep up (Whole Wellness Therapy, 2020). Essentially, your brain is wired to react as if the trauma is happening all over again, even when it's long in the past. There is a lot more going on in your brain when healing from trauma. This helped me to make sense of some of my reactions and feelings. The good news is your brain isn't broken. The brain is essentially a muscle, so you can train and reframe it. Having altered brain activity doesn't mean you won't or can't ever change. It is important to understand how it works so you can utilize the skills in this book to reframe it.

That's why small, everyday stresses can feel like life-or-death situations for trauma survivors. It's not that we're overreacting – it's that our brains are stuck in survival mode. Every argument, every challenge, feels like a direct threat because our brains are still trying to protect us from the trauma we experienced.

Healing from trauma isn't easy, and there's no magic switch that turns it off. It's a process – and, to be honest, it's a long one. But the good news is it's possible. Healing starts with acceptance, and for me, that meant accepting that my trauma was part of my story, but it didn't have to define me. Cognitive-behavioral therapy (CBT) has been shown to be particularly effective in helping individuals reframe negative thoughts and behaviors that result from trauma.[12] CBT utilizes a combination of cognitive therapy and behavioral therapy, so it helps to confront the past while planning for the future.

Talk Therapy

One of the most powerful tools in my healing journey has been talk therapy. Talking about my experiences helped me make sense of the confusion that trauma left behind. Trauma can blur your memories, and it's hard to untangle what happened and how it affected you. A therapist or coach helps guide you through that process, like putting together a puzzle you thought was impossible to solve. Having someone to listen without judgment allowed me to be

---

[12] URMC. (n.d.). *Trauma and mental health: The brain connection.* University of Rochester Medical Center. https://www.urmc.rochester.edu

vulnerable in ways I couldn't be with people in my daily life. Sometimes, it's easier to open up to a stranger than to the people closest to you.

And therapy doesn't have to be traditional. I practice what I call "nature therapy" with my clients. We have counseling sessions while kayaking, hiking, or rock climbing. There's something about being in nature that eases the discomfort of talking about painful things. Talk therapy is about creating a space where healing can happen in a way that feels natural and safe. The important thing is to find someone who can guide you through the process, whatever that looks like for you.

Grounding Technique

One of the most helpful techniques I have learned is grounding. When you are overwhelmed by anxiety or panic, grounding can help bring you back to the present. These grounding techniques help you in moments of emotionally heightened states. They allow you to take a beat and respond differently. Sometimes, the only thing we can control is our response. Grounding allows you to reevaluate the experience before responding, and this can make a huge difference in how you navigate the life around you. There are a couple of techniques I use regularly.

The first is the "3-3-3" technique. In moments of high anxiety, I focus on finding three things I can see, three things I can touch, and three things I can hear. It sounds simple, but it forces your brain to focus on the present moment instead of spiraling into panic. Many people change the number, so you may try five things you can see, four things you can hear, and three things you can smell. The number is not important. You are trying to train your brain to practice mindfulness in the moment. By identifying the things around you, you help your brain refocus on the now.

Another technique is a breathing exercise. Breathing can be a game-changer for all types of anxiety and frustration. When we breathe slowly and control it, our brain and body have time to assess the situation outside the trauma. I breathe in for five seconds, hold for four, and then exhale forcefully for five. This does more than just calm your mind. It actually helps relieve the physical symptoms of anxiety, like the tightness in your chest and shoulders. When your breathing is calm and controlled, your brain interprets that as a signal that you are safe, and your body starts to follow suit. It is simple: when you breathe calmly, your brain gets a signal to start calming down.

These small, simple techniques have made a huge difference in how I respond to stress. And the beauty of grounding is that it's something you can do anywhere, anytime.

Mindfulness and Meditation

Mindfulness and meditation have also been crucial parts of my healing. Every morning, I take a few minutes to meditate and center myself. Meditation isn't about sitting cross-legged and humming – it's about being present with your thoughts. Sometimes, I meditate while hiking or listening to music. The key is to be mindful of what you are feeling, accept it without judgment, and then move on.

In the mornings, I find a quiet spot, put on some instrumental music, and focus on my breathing. If my mind wanders, I gently bring it back to the present. Afterward, I write down any thoughts or emotions that came up during my meditation. This practice helps me start my day from a place of clarity and mindfulness. And with time, I have found that it gets easier. In the beginning, having a guided meditation can be helpful, but eventually, you will learn to do it on your own.

Mindfulness isn't just for moments of meditation, though. It's a practice that can happen anywhere – in traffic, during a conversation, or even while you are making dinner. The more you practice, the more it becomes a part of how you live your life. We will talk more about mindfulness in the next few chapters as we explore emotional intelligence.

The Importance of a Support System

One of the biggest things I learned in my journey is that you can't heal alone. As much as we like to think we can pull ourselves up by our bootstraps, trauma is too heavy to carry by yourself. A good support system – whether it's friends, family, or a Coach – is essential.

I used to be terrified of opening up to people, but I realized that living in fear of vulnerability was holding me back. Once I allowed myself to be honest about my trauma and accepted help, everything started to change. Professional help, in particular, can be a game-changer. A trauma professional can help you sort through the mess of emotions and memories in a way that makes sense.

And if traditional therapy doesn't appeal to you, there are so many alternatives. Online counseling, coaching, group therapy – there's something for everyone. The important thing is to keep looking until you find what works for you.

Remember that healing from trauma isn't an overnight fix. It's a journey, and it's not a straight path. There will be setbacks, bad days, and moments where you feel like you are back at square one. But resilience is built one step at a time.

When Reality Comes Knocking, Face it!

The only way through it is through it. Early on, I tried to take shortcuts. I wanted to feel better now. But I quickly learned that healing takes time, and the only way to truly move forward is to do the work. This can be a challenge and seem an overwhelming task, so be sure to celebrate the small victories along the way. Every time you push through a tough day or make progress, celebrate it. Rewire your brain to seek out the good rather than focusing on the bad.[13] Focus on where you are going. Each step gets you a little closer to the life you want to live.

I also had to learn to forgive myself – and others. Trauma can leave you with a lot of resentment, not just toward the people who hurt you but toward yourself for how you responded. Learning to forgive is one of the most powerful tools in healing. Remember, forgiveness takes time, so utilize the chapter on forgiveness as much as you need. You may find you have to forgive several times, but that's okay.

As I continued on my journey, I realized that I couldn't just avoid my past. For a while, I thought I could heal by focusing only on the present. But my trauma was always there, lurking in the background. It wasn't until I confronted my past head-on that I truly began to heal. It wasn't easy, but it was necessary.

Now, I still have hard days – that's the reality of living with trauma. But I also have the tools to manage it, and so do you! Today, I know that healing is possible. It takes work, but every day brings me closer to the life I want to live.

---

[13] Whole Wellness Therapy. (2020). *Understanding trauma and its impact on mental health*. Whole Wellness Therapy. https://www.wholewellnesstherapy.com

If you are reading this, I want you to know that there's a way through the darkness. You are not alone, and your trauma doesn't have to define you. There's light at the end of this journey – all you have to do is take that first step.

Chapter Five:
Building Self-Esteem and Self-Worth

"The way you talk to yourself matters.
If you tell yourself you are not good enough, you will believe it.
But if you tell yourself you are capable, strong,
and deserving of joy, you will believe that too."

-Anonymous

I used to think self-esteem and self-worth were the same thing. I mean, they sound pretty similar, but I have come to realize that they are like siblings who sometimes get mistaken for each other at family gatherings. Self-esteem is all about how we view our abilities and traits, and it's often shaped by external factors—what we do, what we accomplish, and what others say about us. Self-worth, on the other hand, is a deeper, more personal belief about our value as human beings. It's not tied to what we do but to who we are at our core. And let me tell you; it took me a long time to figure that out.

I struggled with this concept probably longer than anything else in my life. I mean, I used to think that if I messed up at work, it meant I was a complete failure as a person. Or if someone didn't like me, it meant I was unworthy of love. That's a pretty rough way to go through life, and it led me down some dark paths. I spent years in active addiction, trying to numb myself to the pain of not feeling good enough. Even after I got sober, I still carried around this heavy weight of shame and guilt. It was like dragging around a sack full of all my bad decisions, and every time I tried to move forward, it yanked me right back.

But I have learned that self-worth starts from within. It's not something you can earn or achieve. It's something you have to believe about yourself, no matter what's going on around you. And once I started to grasp that, everything began to change.

Understanding The Difference

Let's dive a little deeper. Self-esteem is often tied to what we do. Maybe you are proud of your skills at work or your ability to make people laugh. That's great! But what happens when you mess up a project, or someone doesn't find your jokes funny? If your self-esteem is all you have got, those moments can feel devastating. It's easy to spiral into thinking, "I failed, so I'm a failure." But that's not true. Failing at something doesn't make you a failure. It makes you human.

Self-worth, on the other hand, is about believing that you are valuable just because you exist. It's about knowing, deep down, that you matter—no matter what. You don't have to prove anything to anyone, not even to yourself. You are worthy of love, joy, and success just because you are here.

I know that's easier said than done. When you have been through trauma, abuse, or just a lot of tough times, it can be hard to see yourself as worthy. You start to believe all the negative things people have said about you, or you let your mistakes define you. Trust me, I have been there. After years of addiction and all the things I did during that time, I thought I was beyond redemption. I could forgive everyone else, but I couldn't forgive myself. That voice in my head was relentless, constantly reminding me of everything I'd done wrong.

But you know what? That voice is a liar.

The way we talk to ourselves is crucial. It shapes how we see ourselves and, ultimately, how we show up in the world. If you are always telling yourself, "I'm not good enough," guess what? You are going to start believing it. And if you believe it, you are going to act like it. You will hold yourself back from opportunities, you will settle for less than you deserve, and you will find yourself trapped in a cycle of negativity and self-doubt.

So how do we change that? It starts with recognizing that those negative thoughts aren't the truth. They are just thoughts—powerful ones, sure, but still just thoughts. And you have the power to change them.

I had to learn to talk to myself the way I would talk to a friend. When a friend makes a mistake, you don't say, "Wow, you are such a screw-up. No one's ever going to love you now." No, you'd say, "Hey, you messed up, but it's okay. You're still a good person. You can learn from this." Why not extend the same kindness to yourself?

Simple Ways To Build Self-Worth

One of the best ways I found to change my internal dialogue was to start each day by looking in the mirror and saying something positive. I know it sounds cheesy, but it works. I'd say things like, "I am worthy of love" or "I am capable of doing great things." At first, it felt weird, and I didn't believe it. But the more I did it, the more I started to see that maybe, just maybe, those things were true.

Remember, building self-worth isn't about making grand, sweeping changes overnight. It's about the little things—the small, achievable steps that remind you, day by day, that you are capable, strong, and worthy.

I am going to share a few exercises that have helped me, and I hope they can help you, too. Remember, you don't have to tackle them all at once. Pick one or two to start with and see how they feel. You will be amazed at how even the smallest actions can shift your mindset and help you start seeing yourself in a kinder, more compassionate light.

Set Small, Achievable Goals

When I was at my lowest, everything felt overwhelming. Even basic tasks seemed impossible. But I found that setting small, manageable goals was a game-changer. Start with something really simple—like making your bed every morning or going for a five-minute walk. These might sound trivial, but there's power in small wins. When you complete even the tiniest goal, it sends a signal to your brain that you are capable and that you can follow through. And those little victories add up.

I remember the first time I set a goal to make my bed every morning. It seemed almost laughable—how could such a small act make a difference? But each time I smoothed out the sheets and fluffed the pillows, I felt a sense of accomplishment. I'd look at that neatly made bed and think, *Okay, I did that. What else can I do today?* That momentum carried me through my day, helping me tackle bigger tasks and feel more in control.

So, start small. Set a goal that feels doable and stick to it. Maybe it's drinking a glass of water first thing in the morning or spending five minutes stretching. Whatever it is, make it simple and celebrate when you accomplish it. You deserve that recognition, no matter how small the task may seem.

Practice Gratitude

I know, I know—everyone talks about gratitude like it's some magical cure-all. But the truth is, it really can shift your perspective. When I was deep in my struggle with self-worth, I was laser-focused on what I lacked. I'd obsess over my mistakes, my flaws, all the things I didn't have. But practicing gratitude helped me flip that script.

Every day, I started writing down three things I was grateful for. Sometimes, they were big things, like a supportive friend or a good day at work. But often, they were small—like a beautiful sunset or the way my coffee tasted that morning. And I made sure to include at least one thing about myself. That was the hardest part at first. I'd sit there, staring at the blank page, thinking, *What's good about me?* But slowly, I started to see it. My sense of humor. My resilience. Even just the fact that I got out of bed that day.

Shifting the focus from what you don't have to what you do have—even if it's just the basics—can make a world of difference. It's not about ignoring your struggles; it's about balancing them with the good. So, grab a notebook and jot down three things you are grateful for today. And don't forget to include something about you, because you are worthy of being celebrated.

Clean Up Your Space

I never thought that cleaning up my room would do anything for my mental state. But there's something almost magical about tidying up. When your space is cluttered, it's easy to feel overwhelmed and chaotic. It's like your surroundings are mirroring your mind, and everything just feels messy.

I remember one particularly rough day when I couldn't shake the feeling that I was falling apart. My house was a disaster zone—clothes everywhere, dishes piled up, papers scattered around. I didn't know where to start, but I figured, *Why not start here?* I picked up one thing—a book I'd left on the floor—and put it back on the shelf. Then I folded some clothes and did the dishes, and before I knew it, my place was looking more like a home and less like a war zone.

There is something incredibly empowering about creating order out of chaos, even in a small way. It's a tangible reminder that you have control over something, even if it's just a corner of your room. So, pick one area to tidy up. It doesn't have to be your whole house—maybe just your desk or a drawer. As you clear the clutter, notice how it makes you feel. It's a small act, but it can help shift your mindset from overwhelmed to capable.

Take Care Of Your Appearance

I used to think that taking care of my appearance was just about looking good for others. But I have learned that it's really about showing myself that I am worth the effort. When you are struggling with self-worth, it's easy to let self-care slide. Why bother getting a haircut or wearing something nice if you don't feel like you deserve it?

But the truth is, you do deserve it. Whether it's putting on your favorite outfit, taking a shower, or even just brushing your hair—these small acts of self-care send a powerful message to yourself: *I matter.* It's not about vanity; it's about acknowledging your own worth.

I remember the first time I got a haircut after a particularly tough period. I'd been avoiding it for months, feeling like it wasn't worth the time or money. But when I finally sat in that chair and watched the transformation in the mirror, I felt lighter—not just because of the hair, but because I'd taken that step for myself. It was a small reminder that I was worth the effort.

So, do something for yourself today. It doesn't have to be big—maybe put on your favorite shirt or take a few extra minutes to do something nice for your skin. These little acts of care can have a big impact on how you see yourself.

Stop Comparing Yourself To Others

We all do it, don't we? Scrolling through social media, looking at everyone else's highlight reels, and thinking, *Why can't I have that? Why am I not as successful, happy, or put-together as they are?* It's a trap, and it's one I have fallen into more times than I can count.

But comparing yourself to others is like comparing apples to oranges. Everyone's journey is different, and what you see online is only a fraction of the story. You have no idea what struggles those people are facing behind the scenes. I had to remind myself of this constantly, especially when I was deep in my own struggles.

Focus on being a little better today than you were yesterday. That's it. That's all you need to do. Run your own race at your own pace. When you let go of the need to measure up to others, you free yourself to become the best version of yourself.

The Role Of Material Possessions In Self-Worth

We live in a world where it's easy to get caught up in the idea that having more means being more. A nicer car, a bigger house, a fancy job title—these things can make us feel successful, sure, but they don't define who we are. I used to think that if I just had the right things, people would see me differently, and maybe I'd finally see myself as worthy. But that's a trap.

When you tie your self-worth to what you have, you are setting yourself up for disappointment. Because there's always going to be someone with more, and the moment you get what you want, you start worrying about losing it. It's like trying to fill a bucket with a hole in the bottom—no matter how much you pour in, it's never enough.

I found a lot of peace when I started letting go of that need to have more. Embracing minimalism, focusing on what truly mattered to me, and realizing that I was enough without all the extra stuff—it was freeing. When you stop trying to keep up with everyone else and start living for yourself, you find that you are a lot happier with a lot less.

My Ongoing Journey

Now, I won't pretend I have it all figured out. Self-esteem and self-worth are things I work on every day. There are still moments when that voice in my head tries to convince me that I am not good enough. But I have learned to challenge it, to remind myself that I am worthy just as I am, flaws and all.

One of the biggest lessons I have learned is that it's okay to be a work in progress. You don't have to be perfect to be valuable. You don't have to have it all together to be worthy of love and respect. It's about progress, not perfection. And every step you take toward loving yourself more, even if it's a tiny step, is a victory.

Embrace Who You Are: It's Worth It

There's a delicate balance between self-confidence and arrogance. It's easy to swing from one extreme to the other, especially when you are trying to build yourself up after years of feeling small. I used to be terrified of being arrogant, but I have learned that real confidence isn't about thinking you are better than anyone else. It's about knowing your worth without needing to put others down.

If you are reading this and struggling with your own self-worth, I want you to know that you are not alone. I have been there. I know how dark it can feel when you are convinced that you are not enough. But I also know that you can change that. It won't happen overnight, and it won't always be easy, but it is possible.

Start small. Start with one kind word to yourself each day. Start with one little goal that you can achieve. Start by forgiving yourself for one mistake. And keep going because you are worth it. You really are.

It took me a long time to get here, but I have come to see that self-worth isn't something you achieve once and then keep forever. It's something you build and rebuild, day by day. It's about being honest with yourself, acknowledging your flaws, and choosing to love yourself anyway.

I hope that wherever you are on your journey, you can find a little more kindness for yourself. Because the world needs you exactly as you are, imperfections and all. And you deserve to feel that, to know it, deep down in your bones. You are enough.

The Power of Who We Surround Ourselves With

One of my favorite sayings is, "If you hang out with six successful people, you will become the seventh." It's a simple yet profound reminder that the people we choose to spend time with have an immense impact on our lives. The energy, mindsets, and behaviors of those around us can shape how we see ourselves, how we approach challenges, and even the level of success we achieve.

When you surround yourself with individuals who lift you up, who support your dreams, and who continue to inspire and push you forward, you begin to adopt those same qualities. These are the people who remind you of your strengths when you have lost sight of them, who see potential in you even during moments when you may doubt yourself. These relationships are not only fulfilling but essential for personal growth.

But this influence is not one-sided. It's just as important to be that supportive person for others. By encouraging and believing in the people around you, you not only strengthen those relationships but also reinforce your own sense of purpose and positivity. This reciprocity fosters an environment of mutual growth and success where everyone involved has the potential to thrive.

The people we spend the most time with play a vital role in how we view ourselves and the world around us. Building relationships with those who continue to motivate, support, and inspire us is not just healthy—it's crucial. Surround yourself with people who bring out the best in you, and be intentional about the energy you bring into the lives of others. Ultimately, these connections can be the key to unlocking your fullest potential.

Remember, this isn't about perfection. It's about progress. It's about learning to love yourself a little more each day, to let go of the past, and to embrace who you are right now. You are worthy of all the joy and love this world has to offer simply because you exist. So, go out there and claim it. You've got this.

Chapter Six:
Cultivating Emotional Intelligence

*"Everything can be taken from a man but one thing:
the last of human freedoms—to choose one's attitude
in any given set of circumstances, to choose one's own way."*

–Viktor Frankl

The only real control we have in life is over how we respond to things. That's it. Not how others act, not what happens in the world, but how we choose to react. It's easy to get caught up in situations we can't change, but our power lies in our response. Whether we face challenges, disappointments, or even unexpected joys, the way we decide to handle them shapes our experience.

For me, this was both terrifying and empowering. Terrifying because it meant no more excuses. I couldn't blame my circumstances, my childhood, or the guy who cut me off in traffic for how I felt or acted. But it was also empowering because it meant I had the power to change, grow, and shape my own experience in life. This, my friends, is emotional intelligence—or EQ for short.

The Foundations Of Emotional Intelligence

Emotional intelligence is about being smart with your emotions. It's understanding your feelings and the impact they have on your thoughts, decisions, and relationships. In other words, it's about not letting your emotions run the show. Emotions are like waves; they come and go, often unexpectedly. But just because a wave is strong doesn't mean we have to let it knock us over. Emotional intelligence teaches us to ride the waves instead of being swept away by them.

Emotions are like the engine of a car: powerful and necessary. But we are the drivers. If we don't have control over the wheel, the car could veer off the road, crash, or worse. EQ is what keeps us in the driver's seat, making sure that our emotions don't drive us into a ditch.

The Components Of Emotional Intelligence

Daniel Goleman, a pioneer in the field of emotional intelligence, identifies four key components that form the foundation of this crucial skill. Each component plays a vital role in helping individuals understand and manage their emotions, as well as navigate social relationships with ease and empathy.

Self-awareness is where emotional intelligence begins. It's the ability to recognize and understand your own emotions as they occur. Without this awareness, managing your emotions becomes incredibly difficult. Being self-aware means taking an honest look at how your emotions influence your thoughts and actions. It's like having an internal weather forecast that allows you to anticipate emotional "storms" before they fully hit. This helps you prepare and potentially avoid reactions that could lead to unnecessary conflict or stress. By recognizing your emotions as they arise, you become better equipped to handle situations more thoughtfully and constructively.

Mastering Self-Awareness And Self-Management

Once you have a good grasp on recognizing your emotions, the next step is self-management. This component of emotional intelligence involves controlling your emotional responses. For example, when you are angry or frustrated, self-management helps you resist the temptation to react impulsively or aggressively. It's about staying calm in tense situations and learning to respond in ways that are beneficial rather than harmful. Think of it as navigating rush-hour traffic: even when things are stressful and it feels like everyone around you is losing their cool, self-management helps you keep a steady hand on the wheel, ensuring you don't get swept up in the chaos. This skill is particularly useful in maintaining professionalism and composure in both personal and work environments.

While self-awareness and self-management are more introspective, social awareness extends outward to include the emotions of others. Social awareness is the ability to perceive and understand the emotions and needs of the people around you. This is where empathy comes into play. Social awareness allows you to pick up on non-verbal cues—such as body language and tone of voice—that might give insight into how someone else is feeling, even if they haven't said a word. It's like being able to hear the emotional "music" others are playing. By developing this awareness, you build a deeper understanding of the emotional connections between people, which can enhance communication and strengthen relationships.

The final component, relationship management, is where all the previous skills come together. Managing relationships is about maintaining positive, healthy interactions with others, even when things get difficult. It requires you to manage your own emotions, be socially aware, and apply those skills to navigate interactions in a way that benefits everyone involved. In many ways, relationship management is like tending to a garden. It requires consistent effort— watering the plants, pulling out weeds, and ensuring they receive the right amount of sunlight. With care and attention, the relationship can flourish, providing a space where both parties feel supported and valued. Strong relationship management leads to stronger connections, effective teamwork, and greater trust.

Why Does EQ Matter?

You might be thinking, *Why should I care about emotional intelligence?* Let me ask you this: Do you want to have better relationships, make smarter decisions, and feel more at peace with yourself? Yeah.

People with high EQ are more successful in their careers and personal lives. They are the ones who can stay calm under pressure, navigate conflicts with grace, and build deeper connections with others. Think of it as a secret superpower. It's not as flashy as flying or mind-reading, but it'll get you through life's challenges with much less drama.

I used to think that being successful meant being tough, staying stoic, and never showing vulnerability. Boy, was I wrong? The more I tried to hide my emotions, the more they bubbled up in ways I couldn't control. It was like trying to hold a beach ball underwater— eventually, it's going to pop up and smack you in the face.

Now, I wasn't always like this. In fact, for a long time, I was the opposite of emotionally intelligent. I spent years numbing my feelings with substances, avoiding them, and letting them fester. My emotional range was survival mode or nothing. I believed the world was out to get me, and I let my past traumas dictate my every reaction.

When I began my journey of sobriety, I was hit with a tidal wave of emotions I hadn't dealt with in years. I was angry, scared, anxious—you name it. My emotions were all over the place, and I didn't know how to handle them. I knew something had to change. I couldn't keep living on this emotional rollercoaster.

The first step was learning to pause. Before reacting, before letting my emotions take the wheel, I had to pause and breathe. This might sound simple, but trust me, in the middle of a panic attack or a wave of anger, pausing feels like trying to stop a freight train. But with practice, I found that just a few seconds of controlled breathing made all the difference. It was like hitting the pause button on a movie that was getting too intense.

I started paying attention to the physical sensations that came with my emotions. Was my chest tightening? Was my jaw clenching? Once I learned to recognize these signals, I could use my breathing techniques to calm myself down before the emotion spiraled out of control. It wasn't an overnight fix, but over time, it changed everything.

Mindfulness And Breathing Exercises

Speaking of breathing, let's talk about how powerful mindfulness can be for emotional intelligence. Mindfulness is like the Swiss Army knife of EQ. It's about being present, paying attention to what is happening right now without getting caught up in what could happen or what already did.

For me, mindfulness came through something as simple as a breathing exercise. When I was in the middle of a panic attack or ready to blow up with anger, focusing on my breath for even a few seconds helped ground me. It was like pressing the reset button.

Now, mindfulness doesn't have to be all about sitting cross-legged in a quiet room with incense burning (although, if that's your thing, go for it!). You can practice mindfulness anywhere—while stuck in traffic, on a walk, or even when waiting for your coffee to brew. It's all about training your brain to be aware of the present moment.

When I first started, I couldn't last more than a minute without getting distracted. But like any skill, the more you practice, the better you get. Eventually, I could feel the benefits of mindfulness in every part of my life. It helped me make better decisions, stay calmer in stressful situations, and respond more thoughtfully to others.

The Power Of Empathy

Empathy is an essential part of emotional intelligence, allowing us to connect with others on a deeper level. While most people think of empathy as a single ability, it actually comes in three distinct forms, each serving a unique purpose. Understanding these types of empathy can help you engage with others in a more meaningful and supportive way.

Cognitive empathy is about understanding someone else's perspective intellectually. It involves knowing what another person likes, dislikes, and how they prefer to be treated. This type of empathy doesn't necessarily involve feeling their emotions but instead focuses on grasping their point of view. For instance, you might not feel the same frustration your friend feels during a difficult situation, but cognitive empathy helps you understand why they are upset. This ability is especially helpful in conversations and problem-solving, as it allows you to anticipate how someone else might react or what they might need in a given moment. In essence, cognitive empathy is like stepping into someone else's shoes without necessarily experiencing their emotions firsthand.

Emotional empathy takes it a step further by allowing you to actually feel what another person is experiencing. This type of empathy involves a direct emotional response to someone else's feelings. For example, if you see someone crying, you might feel your own eyes begin to water, or if someone is angry, you may feel a surge of anger yourself. Emotional empathy creates a stronger emotional connection because it goes beyond understanding—it's about sharing an emotional experience. While this type of empathy can be powerful in fostering deep connections, it can also be overwhelming at times, especially if you are highly sensitive to others' emotions. The challenge with emotional empathy is maintaining balance, ensuring that you are supportive without becoming too absorbed in the emotions of others.

Empathetic concern is the final type, and it's about caring for someone on a deeper, more compassionate level. This kind of empathy isn't just about understanding or feeling another person's emotions; it's about genuinely wanting to help them. Empathetic concern drives actions that demonstrate care, whether it's offering support during a tough time, lending a helping hand, or simply being present for someone in need. Unlike sympathy, which can sometimes feel detached or obligatory, empathetic concern stems from a sincere desire to help because you genuinely care about the other person's well-being. This form of empathy plays a vital role in building strong relationships because it shows that your care for others is not just intellectual or emotional—it's practical and heartfelt.

Empathy is a muscle that gets stronger the more you use it. When we are able to empathize with others, we build stronger relationships and create a more compassionate world. It's not about fixing anyone or solving their problems; it's simply about being present for them.

Self-Awareness and Self-Regulation: The Foundation of EQ

When it comes to emotional intelligence, self-awareness is the foundation. It's like looking in the mirror and seeing yourself clearly, without judgment. This can be hard to do. We are often our own worst critics, but emotional intelligence requires that we be brutally honest with ourselves—both about our strengths and our weaknesses.

I have had to face some hard truths about myself on this journey. There were parts of me I wasn't proud of, things I needed to change. But instead of beating myself up about it, I focused on growth. I wasn't aiming for perfection, just progress.

Self-regulation is the next step. Once you are aware of your emotions, the goal is to manage them in a healthy way. This doesn't mean bottling them up or pretending they don't exist. It means finding ways to express them that aren't destructive. For me, it was about setting boundaries, practicing patience, and letting go of the need to always be right.

Techniques For Improving Emotional Intelligence

Improving emotional intelligence (EI) can transform how you handle relationships, deal with stress, and navigate life's daily ups and downs. Emotional intelligence is essentially your ability to recognize and manage not only your own emotions but also the emotions of others. Developing this skill requires conscious effort, but the rewards are significant: better communication, enhanced empathy, and a stronger sense of inner peace. So, where do you start? Here are a few techniques that can help you enhance your emotional intelligence. These methods have been tried and tested and have had a profound impact on many, including myself.

You have likely heard about the importance of breathing, but it's worth emphasizing. When emotions run high—whether it's anger, anxiety, or excitement—your body often reacts with shallow, rapid breaths. This can exacerbate emotional responses, making it harder to stay calm and focused. Controlled breathing exercises are an accessible and powerful way to regulate your body's reaction to stress and emotional triggers.

One of the most effective techniques is deep, diaphragmatic breathing, which involves inhaling deeply into your belly and then exhaling slowly. This type of breathing helps lower your heart rate and reduces the physiological symptoms of stress. By calming your body, your mind becomes clearer, and you are better able to choose your response rather than reacting impulsively.

For instance, when you feel the stirrings of frustration or anger in a conversation, take a few moments to focus on your breath. Inhale deeply through your nose, hold for a few seconds, and then exhale through your mouth. Repeat this cycle for a minute or two. The result is often a sense of calm, which allows you to regain control of your emotions and engage in a more thoughtful and measured way.

Meditation may sound intimidating to some, but it doesn't require a special environment, hours of practice, or even the ability to sit still. At its core, meditation is about giving your mind a break and staying present in the moment. When practiced consistently, meditation can significantly improve your emotional intelligence by helping you develop greater self-awareness, focus, and emotional regulation.

You can meditate almost anywhere. Whether you are taking a hike, cooking dinner, or even driving (just keep your eyes open), moments of mindfulness can arise naturally. When emotions flare, these brief moments of meditation can anchor you, allowing you to observe your feelings without being overwhelmed by them.

For example, if you are dealing with a particularly stressful situation, you might try mindful walking. With each step, notice the sensation of your feet touching the ground, the air around you, or the rhythm of your breathing. This act of mindfulness helps quiet racing thoughts and emotions, grounding you in the present.

Journaling is another technique that fosters emotional intelligence. By writing down your thoughts and feelings, you give yourself the space to process emotions that may otherwise feel overwhelming. It's a bit like having a private conversation with yourself, allowing you to gain clarity, identify patterns in your emotional responses, and find solutions.

Sometimes, emotions are difficult to understand when they are floating around in your head, but once they are written down, they often become clearer. You may begin to notice certain triggers that consistently evoke emotional reactions, such as stress at work or a particular interaction with a friend. By recognizing these patterns, you can better anticipate emotional responses and manage them proactively.

Journaling is particularly helpful when you need to work through complex feelings, such as frustration, sadness, or confusion. For example, after a heated conversation with a colleague, you might journal about what was said, how it made you feel, and why it triggered a strong emotional reaction. This reflection can provide insight into how to handle similar situations in the future, helping you become more emotionally resilient.

When emotions run high, finding small, comforting actions can help you regain control. Self-soothing techniques are simple yet powerful ways to calm your mind and body during emotional turbulence. These practices vary from person to person, but the idea is to engage in something that brings you comfort and a sense of safety.

For some, it might be eating a piece of chocolate, curling up with a book, or taking a warm bath. For others, it could be going for a walk, listening to soothing music, or engaging in a familiar hobby. Personally, I have found that even something as simple as grabbing a fruit roll-up can make a big difference when I am feeling stressed. The key is to find what works for you, something that helps you slow down and shift your emotional state without relying on more harmful coping mechanisms.

Self-soothing is not about avoiding or suppressing emotions but rather giving yourself the space to calm down before processing those emotions in a healthy way. It's like putting on your emotional oxygen mask before you deal with the situation at hand. When you are calm, you can think more clearly and make decisions that align with your long-term emotional well-being.

Pausing before reacting to a situation is one of the most impactful techniques for enhancing emotional intelligence. It's all too easy to let emotions dictate your actions, especially when they are strong. However, learning to pause gives you the opportunity to choose your response rather than reacting impulsively.

Suppose you are in a situation where someone says something that offends or frustrates you. Your initial instinct might be to snap back, but by pausing—even for just a few seconds—you allow yourself to process the emotion and decide how you want to respond. This pause can be transformative. It offers you the chance to ask yourself: "Is this reaction aligned with my values? Will it help or hurt the situation?" In many cases, simply taking a deep breath and waiting a moment can prevent unnecessary conflict and help you engage with others in a more thoughtful way.

Incorporating this practice into your daily life requires mindfulness and self-discipline, but the benefits are profound. Over time, you will find that you are better equipped to handle emotionally charged situations with grace and maturity.

Personal Accountability: Cleaning Your Side Of The Street

One of the most important lessons I learned on this journey is personal accountability. My sponsor used to tell me, "Clean your side of the street." What that means is, in any situation, focus on your part. Take responsibility for your actions and reactions, and don't worry about what the other person did wrong. Apologize when necessary and make amends for your mistakes.

This was hard for me at first because, like most people, I was good at pointing fingers. But the truth is, we can't control anyone else's behavior—only our own. By focusing on my own actions and keeping my side of the street clean, I found a sense of peace and self-worth that I hadn't known before.

The Ripple Effect: Healing Ourselves To Help Others

There's a saying, "Hurt people hurt people." I believe the opposite is true as well: healed people can help heal people. When you work on your emotional intelligence, you are not just improving your own life—you are affecting everyone around you.

I have seen firsthand how practicing emotional intelligence can transform lives. Whether it was helping someone manage their anger, teaching mindfulness to a group of addicts, or showing corporate managers how to handle stress, the impact of emotional intelligence is undeniable.

The truth is emotional intelligence isn't just about personal growth. It's about creating a ripple effect that spreads healing, compassion, and understanding to the people in our lives. It's about showing up as the best version of ourselves so we can lift others up, too.

At the end of the day, emotional intelligence boils down to one thing: freedom. The freedom to choose how we respond in any given situation. The freedom to grow, to change, and to live life on our own terms. It's not always easy, and it's definitely not a quick fix, but it's worth it.

So, the next time you are faced with a situation that triggers an emotional reaction, take a moment to pause. Breathe. Remember that you have the power to choose your response. And in that response lies your freedom.

Chapter Seven:
Embracing Vulnerability

"Vulnerability sounds like truth and feels like courage.
Truth and courage aren't always comfortable,
but they're never weakness."

– Brené Brown

You know, it took me years to realize that vulnerability wasn't something to be ashamed of. Like most people, I always thought it was a weakness, a flaw to be hidden at all costs. Growing up, I felt I had to put on this tough exterior and bury all the messy stuff deep inside. Vulnerability felt like opening the floodgates and letting everyone see the parts of me that I was desperately trying to keep hidden. Who wants to do that, right?

But vulnerability, as uncomfortable as it can be, is where real growth begins. It's the step we often avoid because it's risky. There's this voice inside all of us that says, "If they really knew me, they wouldn't like me," and that's scary. But in reality, vulnerability is where we find our strength. It's where we start peeling back the layers of who we think we should be and getting closer to who we really are.

My Journey To Self-Worth

For most of my life, I spent way too much time creating a version of myself that I thought people would accept. I was so busy curating this persona that I forgot to figure out who I actually was. This habit really took off when I moved to New York for college. Nobody there knew my past, so I saw it as a chance for a fresh start. I thought I could be anyone I wanted to be, and it was tempting to leave all the baggage behind—my childhood traumas, mental health struggles, all of it. But the funny thing about baggage is it doesn't just disappear because you decide to ignore it. It sticks with you, quietly weighing you down, whether you acknowledge it or not.

For years, I was the guy with the best stories. I tried to be everything to everyone, always crafting some narrative that would make me seem cooler and more interesting. But deep down, I was terrified. Terrified that someone might see through the cracks and realize that I wasn't this larger-than-life character I'd built. That I was, in fact, just a scared kid who didn't really know who he was. And that fear was exhausting. I was constantly on edge, worried that my house of cards would come tumbling down.

And, of course, it did. Because that's the thing about living a lie—it's not sustainable. You can't keep up the act forever, and eventually, the truth catches up with you. For me, that moment came after I got sober. Suddenly, I had no more distractions, no more ways to numb the fear and anxiety. I had to confront the fact that I didn't know myself at all. It was terrifying. I remember standing in front of the mirror one day, thinking, "What music do I actually like? Do I dress this way because I like it or because it fits the character I've been playing?"

It felt like starting from scratch, and in many ways, it was. I had to re-learn who I was, what I enjoyed, what mattered to me. It was overwhelming, but it was also an incredible opportunity. Vulnerability wasn't just something I had to endure—it became the doorway to discovering myself. I started trying new things, opening myself up to experiences I'd been too scared to explore. I learned to be honest with myself and others, and slowly but surely, I began to build a life that was real.

The truth is embracing vulnerability is scary because it means letting go of control. It's admitting that we are flawed, that we don't have it all together, and that sometimes we'll mess up. And sure, people might judge us for it. But when we hide behind a facade, we rob ourselves of the opportunity to form real connections. We end up living in isolation, even when we are surrounded by people.

What Is Vulnerability?

One of the most profound shifts for me was realizing that vulnerability isn't just about sharing the messy parts of our past—it's about being open in the present. It's about being brave enough to say, "This is who I am, flaws and all." And when we do that, something amazing happens. We start attracting people who accept us, not in spite of our flaws but because of them.

Now, I won't lie to you—being vulnerable isn't easy. In fact, it's one of the hardest things I have ever done. It meant going to people I'd hurt and admitting that I'd lied, that I wasn't the person they thought

I was. It meant owning up to my mistakes and asking for forgiveness, not just from them, but from myself. And let me tell you, that's a tough pill to swallow. There were days when I thought, "Why even bother? It's too late to fix this." But the freedom that came on the other side of those uncomfortable conversations was worth every ounce of discomfort.

It's easy to think that vulnerability makes us weak, but the truth is it's the strongest thing we can do. It takes real courage to open up, to let people see the parts of us we have kept hidden. And once we do, we discover that we are not as fragile as we thought. In fact, we are stronger because of our flaws, not in spite of them.

I remember going to a wedding a few years ago and watching the groom surrounded by his childhood friends. There were seven groomsmen, all of whom had known him since elementary school. As I watched them laugh and celebrate together, I couldn't help but feel a pang of regret. I thought about all the friendships I'd lost over the years, all the connections I'd sabotaged because I was too scared to be real. For so long, I had convinced myself that if people knew the real me, they wouldn't want to stick around. But in trying to avoid rejection, I'd created exactly what I feared—loneliness.

The biggest lesson I have learned is that vulnerability isn't about being perfect. It's about showing up, flaws and all, and trusting that we're enough just as we are. It's about giving ourselves permission to be human. And yes, that means we might get hurt. But it also means we get to experience the joy of real connection, the kind of relationships that are built on honesty and trust.

If you are like me, you have probably spent a lot of time hiding parts of yourself. Maybe you have built walls to protect yourself from getting hurt, and those walls have become so familiar that the idea of tearing them down feels impossible. But what I can tell you is the walls might keep out the pain, but they also keep out the joy. They keep out the love, the laughter, and the deep connections that make life worth living.

Vulnerability is the key to unlocking all of that. It's the courage to let people see you as you are, without the filters or the facade. It's about saying, "This is me, and I'm okay with that." And when you can do that, you'll find that the world responds in kind. You'll attract the kind of relationships that are based on mutual honesty and respect, and you'll start to feel a sense of freedom that you never knew was possible.

So, if you're ready to start embracing vulnerability, remember that you don't have to open up to everyone all at once. Find one person you trust and share something real with them. It doesn't have to be your deepest, darkest secret—just something honest. Then, pay attention to how it feels. Notice the relief that comes with not having to pretend. Notice the way your relationships start to shift and how they become more authentic and more meaningful.

The path to vulnerability isn't a straight line. It's messy, and it takes time. But if you stick with it, I promise you'll start to see changes—not just in your relationships, but in how you feel about yourself. You'll start to realize that you don't have to be perfect to be loved. You just have to be you.

Fear Of Rejection

One of the most common fears I hear from people when they start thinking about opening up is the fear of rejection or failure. It's a universal experience—we are all afraid of looking foolish, of trying and not succeeding, of being laughed at or dismissed. And it's a powerful fear. I spent years of my life avoiding opportunities avoiding relationships, all because I didn't want to risk failing. That fear can feel suffocating, like a weight that sits on your chest and convinces you that playing it safe is the only way to survive.

But that fear is just a part of our brain trying to keep us safe. It remembers every time we have been hurt, every moment of embarrassment, every rejection. The brain is great at holding onto the negative stuff because it wants to protect us from experiencing it again. What it's not so great at is remembering the successes, the wins, and the joy that followed the moments when we dared to take a risk. And so, we end up stuck in a loop where the fear of failure becomes a self-fulfilling prophecy. We don't try because we are afraid of failing, and by not trying, we guarantee that we won't succeed.

One of the first things I had to do in my own journey was to confront that fear head-on. I had to ask myself, "What's the worst that could happen?" And really play it out. What if I gave a talk and nobody liked it? What if I shared my story and people laughed? Sure, it would sting. But would it break me? No. And the more I thought about it, the more I realized that the worst-case scenario wasn't nearly as bad as I'd made it out to be in my mind. The brain is a funny thing like that—it magnifies our fears and downplays our resilience.

So, if you are struggling with the fear of rejection or failure, I'd encourage you to do the same. Take a moment and really think through your worst fear. What would happen if you failed? And then ask yourself, "But what if it goes right?" We spend so much time worrying about what could go wrong that we forget to consider the possibility of success. What if you put yourself out there, and it worked? What if people responded with kindness, acceptance, and love? It's a powerful shift in thinking, and it's one that can help you move past the fear and take that first step.

Vulnerability Let's You Know Yourself Better

Another thing I've learned is that vulnerability isn't just about how we show up for others—it's about how we show up for ourselves. One of the most profound benefits of leaning into vulnerability is that it forces us to get to know ourselves on a deeper level. When we stop pretending to be someone we're not, we create space to discover who we really are. And that can be scary. It's not always easy to confront the parts of ourselves that we've been hiding, the flaws we've been trying to cover up. But it's necessary if we want to grow.

For a long time, I was stuck in what I call "survival mode." I had built such high walls around myself that I wasn't just keeping out the bad stuff—I was keeping out the good stuff, too. Experiences that could have brought me joy, relationships that could have brought me connection—I missed out on so much because I was too afraid to be open. Vulnerability, as I've come to understand it, is about tearing down those walls. It's about saying, "I'm worthy of experiencing the good in life, even if it means I might get hurt along the way."

And let me tell you, when you start letting down those walls, amazing things happen. You start trying new things. You stop holding yourself back. You take risks, not because you're guaranteed success but because you've realized that the adventure of trying is worth it, no matter the outcome. When I stopped pretending to be someone I wasn't, I found that I was actually a lot more capable than I'd given myself credit for. I discovered strengths and talents that I didn't know I had. But more importantly, I discovered that it's okay not to be good at everything. It's okay to try something and fail because every failure is an opportunity to learn more about yourself.

That's another thing people get wrong about vulnerability. They think it's about exposing your weaknesses, but it's really about discovering your strengths. When you are open and honest with yourself, you start to realize that you are stronger than you ever imagined. And when you do, you'll find that the world doesn't collapse around you. In fact, it opens up in ways you never thought possible.

Vulnerability Can Transform Relationships.

One of the biggest changes I noticed when I started embracing vulnerability was how my relationships transformed. For years, I had kept people at arm's length, afraid that if they got too close, they'd see the cracks in my armor. I was so busy trying to impress everyone that I never let anyone really know me. But once I started being honest— once I stopped pretending—I found that the connections I made were deeper, more meaningful. People responded to my authenticity in ways I never expected. And the best part is I didn't have to work so hard to maintain those relationships. There's a kind of freedom that comes with being your true self. You don't have to keep track of lies; you don't have to remember the stories you've told to impress others. You can just be.

Of course, vulnerability isn't a one-time thing. It's not like you open up once, and then you're done. It's a practice, something you have to work on every day. And sometimes, it can feel like nothing's happening. You might be putting yourself out there, and it feels like you're not getting anywhere. But I promise you, if you stick with it, you'll start to see changes—both in yourself and in how you relate to the world.

There will be setbacks. Not everyone will respond the way you hope. Some people may judge you; some relationships may fall apart. But that's okay. Vulnerability isn't about pleasing everyone—it's about being true to yourself. And the relationships that matter, the ones built on honesty and trust, are the ones that will last. They're worth the risk.

So, how do you start? You start by being brave. It doesn't have to be a huge, life-altering change. You don't have to share your deepest secrets with the world all at once. Start small. Be honest in a conversation where you might normally hold back. Admit when you are struggling instead of pretending everything's fine. And most importantly, be kind to yourself. Vulnerability is hard, and it's okay to take it one step at a time.

One of the things that helped me the most was learning to apologize. I used to be terrified of admitting when I was wrong, but I've found that there's real power in owning up to your mistakes. Apologizing doesn't make you weak—it makes you stronger. It shows that you are willing to take responsibility for your actions and make things right. And in doing so, you give others permission to do the same.

Vulnerability also means reflecting on your behavior and being willing to look at the parts of yourself that need improvement. I used to be a terrible listener. I was so wrapped up in my own world that I didn't really hear what other people were saying. It wasn't until I started reflecting on my interactions that I realized how much I was missing. So, I made a conscious effort to listen more so as to be present in my conversations. And that small change made a huge difference in my relationships.

At the end of the day, vulnerability is about connection. It's about showing up fully, without hiding and allowing others to do the same. When you are vulnerable, you give others permission to be vulnerable, too. It's contagious. And that's how we build real, lasting relationships—by being brave enough to be ourselves.

So, here's my challenge to you: Start today. Take one small step toward vulnerability. It doesn't have to be perfect, and it won't always be easy. But I promise you, it will be worth it. You'll start to see yourself differently. You'll start to see the people around you differently. And little by little, you'll begin to build a life that feels more authentic, more real, and more fulfilling.

You're stronger than you think. You've got this.

Chapter Eight:
Living With Purpose And Meaning

*"The two most important days in your life
are the day you are born, and the day you find out why."*

–Mark Twain

Finding out why we are here is what gives us direction. It's like knowing which road to take when you have been driving around lost for what feels like forever. Purpose is, in the simplest sense, the reason something exists. But when we apply that to life, it's the reason *you* exist. Purpose is what gives your life meaning. It's your guide when you are unsure and your fuel when the journey feels tough. Purpose isn't some giant, unmovable thing you have to figure out right away. It's something you discover little by little, like unwrapping a gift packed in several layers.

The Essence Of Purpose: Defining Meaning In Life

When I talk about purpose, I am not just talking about lofty goals like ending world hunger or becoming the next big thing. Sure, those are amazing ambitions, but purpose is more personal than that. It's about what makes you feel alive, what makes you want to get out of bed in the morning. It could be raising a family, creating art, helping others, or even learning something new. And the best part is your purpose doesn't have to stay the same. It grows with you. As you change, your purpose shifts and adapts, and that's totally okay.

I remember a time when my only purpose was to survive the day. That was it. Just make it through 24 hours without losing myself to my addictions. And you know that was enough. Sometimes, your purpose for the moment is just to survive. And there's no shame in that. The purpose isn't always glamorous, but it's always essential.

If you are anything like I was, you might think finding your purpose means sitting down, writing out some grand vision for your life, and then sticking with it forever. But that's not how it works. The purpose is a journey, not a one-time destination. It's something you uncover over time as you learn more about yourself, forgive yourself for past mistakes, and open yourself up to new experiences.

Purpose As A Journey, Not A Destination

At the beginning of my recovery, I thought my purpose had to be something huge, something that would make up for all the mistakes I'd made. But the truth is, purpose doesn't need to be enormous. It can be simple, and it should be about what resonates with *you*. It's personal. For me, at first, my purpose was just staying sober and keeping my life together. That was enough of a challenge on its own! I wasn't thinking about five years down the road or what grand things I'd accomplish. I was focused on today, on what I could do right now. And honestly, that's where I think purpose begins for most of us—in the now.

There's no magical moment where everything clicks, and you suddenly know what your purpose is for the rest of your life. It changes and evolves. Sometimes, your purpose for the day is just to get out of bed and put one foot in front of the other. And that's okay. There's no rush to have it all figured out.

When life gets confusing or overwhelming (and believe me, it will), having a sense of purpose helps. It's like having a compass when you're lost in a forest. You might not know exactly where you're going, but it gives you some sense of direction. Purpose isn't about perfection; it's about progress.

The Purpose Isn't About Perfection; It's About Progress.

I can't tell you how many times I've felt lost. Even now, with all the work I've done, there are days when I feel like I'm just fumbling through life. But when I get off track, I remind myself of what I'm here to do. I go back to my purpose—helping people, showing up for those in pain, being there for others—and it pulls me back on the path. It's like a reset button for the mind. It gives me the clarity I need when I feel overwhelmed by everything else.

Purpose doesn't just give you direction; it gives you energy. When you are living in alignment with your purpose, you're fueled by something bigger than yourself. It's like running on a different kind of fuel, one that doesn't burn out so easily. That doesn't mean you won't get tired. You will. I do. But purpose gives you the strength to keep going even when the road gets hard.

One of the most important lessons I've learned about purpose is that it's not just about me. Sure, purpose is deeply personal, but it's also about how you fit into the bigger picture. How do your talents, your passions, and your strengths help the world around you? That's where the magic happens.

I'm not saying you have to become a superhero or change the entire world. But think about the little ways your purpose can ripple out and impact the people around you. Maybe it's being a great parent, showing up for your friends when they need support, or using your talents to help others heal. It doesn't have to be grand, but it should be meaningful.

For me, that realization came when I started working with other people in recovery. In the beginning, I was just trying to get through my own struggles, but as I began to heal, I realized I had something to offer. My experiences—my pain, my mistakes, my lessons—could actually help other people. And that's when I really started to feel connected to my purpose. I wasn't just surviving anymore; I was thriving because I was helping others.

Purpose Helps You Make A Difference

Living with purpose is especially important when you're healing from something—whether that's trauma, addiction, or just the general ups and downs of life. Purpose gives you something to focus on outside of your pain. It's like a light at the end of the tunnel, pulling you forward even when things feel dark.

I know from experience how easy it is to get stuck in your own head, especially when you're hurting. When I was going through the worst of my addiction, it felt like I was the only person in the world going through that kind of pain. But when I started to live, I realized that I wasn't alone. My purpose helped me connect with others who were struggling, and that connection was healing.

Purpose doesn't erase pain, but it does give it context. It helps you see that your struggles aren't the end of the story—they're just part of the journey. And when you can take that step back and look at the bigger picture, it makes it easier to keep going.

Purpose Begins With Self-Reflection

So, how do you even start to find your purpose? It begins with self-reflection. Ask yourself: What excites you? What makes you feel alive? What are you naturally good at? And maybe just as important—what frustrates you? Sometimes, the things that upset us the most point us toward the work we're meant to do.

When I first started reflecting on my own purpose, I thought about what made me tick. I realized that I felt the most alive when I was helping others, particularly those who had been through similar struggles. That realization didn't come all at once, though. It took time. I had to try different things, talk to different people, and experience new situations to figure out what truly mattered to me. And that's how it will probably be for you, too.

One of the biggest components of purpose is service—how you use your gifts to help the world around you. It's not about being selfless or putting others ahead of yourself in an unhealthy way. It's about realizing that you have something unique to offer and finding ways to share that with the world.

For me, it was working with other addicts, coaching people who were struggling, and helping them find the tools they needed to heal. That's where I found my joy. And the more I did it, the more I realized that my purpose wasn't just about me—it was about the people I could help.

So, take a moment to think about the ways you can serve. It doesn't have to be anything big or dramatic. It could be as simple as using your talents to bring a little more joy into the world. Those small acts of service add up, and they're often where we find the greatest sense of purpose.

If all of this feels overwhelming, remember that you're not alone. Finding your purpose is a process, and there's no rush to figure it all out right away. Start with what you know today, and take one step at a time. Some days, that step might be small—just getting through the day. And that's okay. As long as you're moving forward, you're on the right track.

And if you're struggling with figuring out what your purpose is, take a deep breath. You don't have to have all the answers. Sometimes, it's enough just to ask the questions. Your purpose will unfold as you keep asking, keep reflecting, and keep growing.

If you've made it this far, congratulations! Seriously. Just thinking about purpose can be an exhausting process, and the fact that you're here means you're already on your way to something better. It's not always easy to dig into these big questions, and it's completely normal to feel a bit lost or uncertain. I felt that way for years, and some days, I still do.

So, let's find the practical side of things: how do you actually go about finding your purpose? If you're sitting there thinking, *That sounds great, but where do I start?*, you're not alone. The good news is that there are plenty of ways to begin discovering what drives you and how to make it part of your daily life.

Before we get into finding purpose, let's talk about why it's important. You might be wondering why everyone makes such a big deal out of this idea of purpose. Is it really necessary to live a fulfilling life? Can't you just coast along and see where life takes you?

Sure, you can do that. But in my experience, life without purpose tends to feel a bit like you're just drifting from one thing to the next without any real direction. And while that might feel fine for a while, it eventually leads to a sense of dissatisfaction. You start wondering what it's all for.

I've been there. Before I found my purpose, I was basically just reacting to life. I wasn't planning, I wasn't pursuing anything meaningful—I was just getting through the day. And while that might sound like an okay strategy, it didn't make me feel alive. It didn't give me a reason to push myself or to grow. When you have a purpose, everything starts to click into place. You feel as if life suddenly has a point, a direction, and you're not just floating aimlessly anymore.

Now, if you're thinking that you need to have this big, grand purpose right away, I'm going to stop you right there. The purpose is not about having it all figured out. In fact, you'll never be completely done with it. It's something you work on every single day. It evolves as you do.

Even now, I don't have my purpose all figured out. I still take it one day at a time, and my purpose continues to shift as I grow. The important thing is that I keep moving forward, keep reflecting on what drives me, and adjust when necessary.

You don't have to know your "ultimate purpose" right away. In fact, you probably never will. Instead, think of purpose as something that's fluid, something that can change and adapt as you do. And that's what makes it exciting—your purpose isn't set in stone. It's a living, breathing thing that grows with you.

So, how do you start figuring out what your purpose is? One word: *reflection*.

You've got to take the time to look inward and ask yourself some important questions. What makes you tick? What gets you excited? What are you naturally good at? And maybe, most importantly, what frustrates you? Sometimes, the things that bother you the most are the things you're meant to work on.

For example, I've always been deeply frustrated by how addiction devastates families. It's something I experienced personally, and it's something that still makes me angry when I see it happening to others. That frustration is part of what drives me to do the work I do today— helping people break free from addiction and rebuild their lives.

It wasn't always obvious to me, though. I didn't just wake up one day and say, "Oh, this is my purpose!" It took years of self-reflection, trial and error, and a whole lot of failure before I really started to understand what my purpose was. And even now, it's still evolving. But that's the beauty of it—the purpose isn't a one-time discovery. It's something you uncover bit by bit.

So, take some time to reflect. Think about the things that light you up and the things that bring you down. Somewhere in there is a clue to your purpose.

Something that might surprise you is purpose isn't just about what you want. It's about how you can serve others.

I know, I know—*"But isn't purpose supposed to be about my personal fulfillment?"* Yes and no. Yes, you should absolutely feel fulfilled by your purpose, but real fulfillment comes from helping others. I've found that the more I focus on serving the people around me, the more purpose and meaning I feel in my own life.

We're all connected in some way, whether we realize it or not. The things we do—big or small—ripple out and impact the people around us. When you start living with purpose, you're not just improving your own life; you're making a difference in the lives of others.

If you're feeling overwhelmed by the idea of finding your purpose, that's okay. Start small. Focus on what you can do *today*. What's one small step you can take toward living with more meaning? Maybe it's something as simple as listening to a new podcast, trying something new, or reflecting on what makes you feel alive. You don't have to figure it all out at once. Just take one step at a time.

The good thing is that purpose grows as you do. As you take those small steps, you'll start to uncover more about yourself and what drives you. Before you know it, those small steps will add up to something much bigger.

If there's one thing I want you to take away from this chapter, it's this: it's okay not to have all the answers right now. You don't need to have your entire purpose figured out today or even tomorrow. This is a process, and it takes time.

I spent years feeling lost, unsure of what I was supposed to be doing with my life. But looking back, I can see that even in those moments of uncertainty, I was still moving forward. Every step, no matter how small, was leading me closer to discovering my purpose. And that's how it works for all of us.

You don't have to be perfect. You don't have to have all the answers. You just have to keep moving forward, keep asking the right questions, and keep showing up. The purpose will come when you're ready for it.

Now that we've explored what purpose is and how to start finding it let's talk about how to *live* it. Knowing your purpose is only part of the journey—living it, breathing it, and letting it guide your everyday life is where the real work begins. And trust me, it's not always easy, but it's worth it.

Once you have a clearer sense of what your purpose might be, it's important to start turning that sense of direction into action. And how do we do that? With goals. Not just any goals, though. I'm talking about goals that actually matter to you—goals that align with your purpose and help you move closer to living the life you want.

They give you something to aim for, something concrete to work toward. Without them, your purpose can feel a little too abstract. But with goals, you break that big, meaningful purpose down into smaller, achievable steps.

Think of it like hiking up a mountain. You wouldn't just leap from the bottom to the top in one giant step, right? No, you'd take it one step at a time, stopping to rest when needed but always keeping your eyes on the path ahead. And that's what goals do for you—they keep you focused on the next step rather than overwhelming yourself with the enormity of the journey.

Set SMART Goals

Now, when it comes to setting goals, it's important to make sure they're realistic and actionable. That's where the SMART framework comes in handy. SMART goals are:

- Specific: Be clear about what you want to accomplish. Instead of saying, "I want to be healthier," say, "I want to exercise three times a week."

- Measurable: You need to be able to track your progress. How will you know when you've achieved your goal? Make it quantifiable.

- Attainable: This is where you check in with reality. Can you reasonably achieve this goal with the resources and time you have?

- Relevant: Your goals should align with your purpose and values. They need to matter to *you*.

- Timed: Set a deadline. Without a time frame, it's easy to keep pushing things off. Give yourself a target date to complete the goal.

Let me tell you a story about how SMART goals helped me in my own journey. When I first decided that I wanted to work as a counselor, it felt impossible. I was in my 30s, had no formal education beyond high school, and the idea of going back to school while juggling work and family felt overwhelming. But I broke it down. I set small, specific goals for each step of the way: apply for one class, then pass that class, then take the next. One step at a time, I climbed that mountain.

And each small goal felt achievable. I wasn't thinking about the entire journey; I was just focused on the step right in front of me. And that's what I encourage you to do: break it down. You don't need to have the whole path figured out. You just need to know the next step.

Living with purpose is a lot like maintaining a garden. You don't just plant the seeds and walk away, hoping everything works out. You have to tend to it regularly—water it, pull out the weeds, and make sure it's getting enough sunlight. Your purpose works the same way. You have to nurture it, stay aligned with it, and be mindful of when things start to drift.

One of the most helpful tools I've found for staying aligned with my purpose is something incredibly simple: *gratitude*. Taking time to reflect on the things you're grateful for each day helps you stay connected to your purpose, especially when life gets tough. When you're stressed, frustrated, or feeling overwhelmed, it's easy to lose sight of why you're doing what you're doing. Gratitude brings you back to the center.

When I'm feeling burnt out or like I've taken on too much, I sit down and reflect on how far I've come. I think about the people I've helped, the growth I've experienced, and the small wins along the way. Gratitude helps me remember why I started this journey in the first place, and it gives me the energy to keep going.

I also make it a point to revisit my goals regularly and check in with myself. Am I still on track? Are my actions still aligned with my purpose? If not, what needs to change? This kind of self-reflection is crucial because life has a funny way of throwing distractions at us. Staying focused requires regular check-ins to make sure you're still heading in the right direction.

One of the hardest parts of living with purpose is finding the balance between pursuing long-term goals and enjoying the present moment. Sometimes, you'll need to give up immediate pleasure for future gains. But that doesn't mean you have to live a life of sacrifice. It's about finding joy in the journey, not just the destination.

There were plenty of times when I wanted to quit school and just focus on making more money in the short term. After all, who doesn't want to feel comfortable and secure? But, I knew that the long-term satisfaction of living my purpose as a counselor would be worth the temporary discomfort. And I was right.

That said, it's important not to deprive yourself of joy along the way. Purpose isn't just about work; it's about finding balance. Make time for the things that fill your bucket, whether that's spending time with loved ones, enjoying your hobbies, or simply relaxing. Living with purpose doesn't mean burning yourself out—it means living fully.

I wish I could tell you that once you find your purpose, everything will fall into place, and life will be smooth sailing. But you and I both know that's not how life works. There will be challenges, setbacks, and moments when you doubt everything. And that's okay.

What will keep you going through those tough times is your purpose. Purpose gives you the resilience to face challenges head-on, knowing that the struggle is part of the process. It's what helps you get back up when life knocks you down.

I've had plenty of moments where I wanted to throw in the towel. There were days when the weight of everything felt like too much—days when I questioned if I was really cut out for the path I had chosen. But every time, my purpose pulled me through. It reminded me that there was something bigger at stake, something worth fighting for.

Purpose As An Anchor During Life's Tough Times

You might be going through your own tough time right now. Maybe you're dealing with personal challenges, health issues, financial stress, or relationship problems. Whatever it is, remember this: your purpose can be your anchor. It's not going to make the hard stuff disappear, but it will give you the strength to push through.

As we wrap up this chapter, I want to leave you with this thought: purpose is not a finish line. It's not something you figure out once, and then you're done. It's a lifelong journey, one that will continue to evolve as you do.

There will be times when your purpose feels crystal clear and other times when it feels murky and confusing. That's normal. What's important is that you keep showing up. Keep asking yourself the big questions. Keep reflecting on what drives you. Keep taking those small steps, even when the path ahead feels unclear.

And most of all, be kind to yourself. Living with purpose isn't about being perfect. It's about making the effort every day to align your life with what matters most to you. Some days that will mean making huge strides forward. On other days, it will mean just getting through. Both are valid, and both are part of the process.

At the end of the day, living with purpose is about more than just setting goals or achieving success. It's about creating a life that feels meaningful to *you*. It's about knowing that your time here matters and that the things you do—no matter how small—make a difference.

So, start small. Reflect on what lights you up, what frustrates you, and what you're naturally good at. Set goals that align with your purpose, and take things one step at a time. Most importantly, remember that your purpose will grow and change with you. You don't need to have all the answers right now. Just keep moving forward, keep asking the right questions, and keep showing up.

You're stronger than you realize.

Chapter Nine:
Practicing Gratitude And Mindfulness

"These mountains that you are carrying,
you were only supposed to climb."

—Najwa Zebian

Life can feel like one endless backpacking trip where we load up with everything — the good, the bad, and especially the heavy stuff. But the thing is, so much of that weight isn't even meant to be carried. It's there for us to learn from and move past, but instead, we often keep it strapped on, lugging it through every situation and interaction. Practicing mindfulness and gratitude has shown me that we don't have to carry it all; we can take what we need from each experience and leave the rest behind.

Think that your brain is like a snow globe. Shake it up, and all those little flakes of snow represent your thoughts—racing around, bumping into each other, sometimes completely clouding your view.

Mindfulness is like putting the snow globe down. The snow doesn't disappear, but it settles. Suddenly, you can see clearly through the glass. The chaos is still there, but it's not overwhelming anymore. That's what mindfulness does—it helps everything settle so you can respond, not react.

Practice Mindfulness To Let Go Of Worries

I know mindfulness might sound like something you hear about all the time, but there's a reason it's been woven into every part of this journey. Mindfulness is the foundation for nearly every other step in healing. It's about simply being present — experiencing each moment as it is, without judgment. Instead of trying to shove away our thoughts or deny what's going on, we learn to accept it. This doesn't mean letting the world walk all over us or ignoring our goals and values. It's about dropping the mental fight against what *is* so that we can actually deal with it.

When you are in the moment, letting go of tomorrow's fears or yesterday's regrets, you can fully experience what's happening right now. And it means training yourself to experience each moment without letting judgment or knee-jerk reactions take over. Remember when we talked about accepting reality? That's mindfulness in action. You focus on the here and now without dragging in your whole history or expectations of the future.

Mindfulness also gives us a chance to respond instead of react. So often, we let a quick reaction take over, only to feel less than proud afterward. But when we make mindfulness a regular part of life, it's like adding a pause button to our minds. We can stop, take a breath, and respond in a way that feels true to ourselves. If we do this long

Joshua Barrett

enough, we're more at peace — able to enjoy the good stuff fully and work through the tough stuff with a clearer mind.

When we practice mindfulness regularly, peace starts to feel more natural. You begin to worry less, panic less, and handle whatever comes your way with a little more patience. You start living in the present instead of waiting for the next moment to solve all your problems or for the last one to define your day. Imagine you're a musician tuning your instrument — mindfulness is like keeping your inner self in tune so you can handle whatever life decides to play.

It doesn't mean you won't feel stress or frustration. Those are part of life, too. But with mindfulness, you have a tool that helps you feel more in control of your reactions. You'll find it easier to focus on the now without dragging in anger from a past moment or fear about the future. This is huge when it comes to interacting with others. If I bring every bit of past pain into each new interaction, I'm responding to today's situation with yesterday's emotions. But when I'm mindful, I can respond to what's actually happening with empathy and a clear mind.

I think our emotions are like scars from past pain. If we don't address them, they start to color the way we see the world and the people in it. With mindfulness, we can clear away that layer and see each moment for what it really is.

Focus On The Good

If mindfulness is about being present, then gratitude is about noticing what's good in that moment. And it doesn't have to be grand gestures or big life changes. It can be as simple as appreciating your morning coffee, a friendly smile, or the quiet moment before everyone

90

else wakes up. Gratitude doesn't need drama; it's an intentional shift in focus from what's wrong to what's right.

When you've been through a lot, gratitude can feel forced or even silly. But I've found it's like training a muscle. We're naturally wired to remember the negative — it's part of our survival instinct. Ask a group to list what went wrong this week, and they'll rattle off a dozen things. But ask them to share one good thing. That takes longer. It's leftover survival programming that doesn't always serve us well now.

Gratitude gives us the tools to see a softer side of life. It helps us move from survival mode to a more balanced place where we notice the small blessings around us. When we make it a habit, we start to realize that joy isn't something that's out there waiting to be found; it's right here, often hiding in plain sight. All it takes is a little attention.

I started with the basics: writing down three things I'm grateful for every morning. At first, it was pretty simple stuff — coffee, running water, my dog. But over time, I found myself digging deeper, really looking for things I appreciated. That changed my whole attitude. I began to notice that I was calmer, less anxious, and more able to let things go. When I skipped my gratitude practice, I felt it; I was more on edge less patient. But when I kept it up, everything felt lighter, and the good in life became more obvious.

Now, gratitude isn't just something I write down — I try to live it. I make a point of calling out the beauty I see in others, whether it's a kind gesture or a thoughtful comment. It's created genuine connections and trust because people can sense when you're genuinely appreciative. It's like my whole outlook shifted from looking for the negative to seeking out the good.

Research backs this up, too. Gratitude can lower the risks of depression, anxiety, and even substance abuse. People who practice gratitude regularly also tend to be more patient and better at making decisions. Mindfulness has equally powerful benefits; it helps us cope with pain, lowers stress, and gives us a better handle on our emotions. And it even affects how our brain works — making us more resilient and better at processing experiences without letting old scars dictate our reactions.

Make Gratitude And Mindfulness
A Mandatory Part Of Your Routine

Gratitude and mindfulness are like mental exercises. The more we do them, the stronger those neural pathways become. Soon, it's not just a practice — it's our default setting, the way we experience life. We become more open to the joy, better equipped to handle the setbacks, and able to face each day with a little more peace.

Let's talk routines because they're what keep all of this going. Here's what my day looks like, though yours doesn't have to be the same. The idea is to find what works for you and then build on it.

1. Morning Gratitude: I start my day by splashing a little cold water on my face; I heard Jason Bateman do it, and that is all I needed. However, there is real science behind it, I promise. Cold water is great for our nerves and blood flow, and I have found the practice is more efficient than coffee in waking me up. It has become a great way to let my body know I am ready for the day. I also jot down three things I'm grateful for. It's a small thing, but it sets a positive tone for the day and gets my mind in a good place.

2. Mindful Moments: I take my dogs for a walk, and during that time, I stay present. I notice the sounds, the smells, and even the cool morning air. It's a way to start the day without distraction and just be.

3. Afternoon Reset: Around midday, I'll take a few minutes to breathe and reflect. If the day's been rough, it's a way to reset and keep going. Sometimes, I'll even jot down a few more things I'm thankful for just to stay focused on the good.

4. Evening Reflection and Gratitude: Before bed, I write down anything that stands out from the day. It could be a lesson, a funny moment, or just something that went well. I spent a few minutes reflecting on how I could have handled things better — not to beat myself up, but to keep growing.

Every night, I spend a few minutes reflecting on my day — not to beat myself up, but to genuinely look at how I handled things. I think about those moments where my reaction maybe wasn't the best. Why did I react that way? What triggered me? And most importantly, how could I respond differently next time? This isn't about dwelling on what went wrong but about seeing where I can make small tweaks.

It's kind of like checking your daily scorecard, not to see if you're "winning" or "losing," but to notice how things played out. If I keep noticing the same reactions in similar situations, I know it's worth paying attention to. And, if you're worried this sounds like a downer before bed, don't be. I always follow it up with a few moments of gratitude to end the day on a good note. This way, I'm focused on growth without losing sight of what's good in my life.

I know routines sound boring to some people, but they're truly helpful. My whole reflection, reading, and gratitude practice takes about an hour, but it's spread throughout the day. For example, I spend about 30 minutes reading, doing 10-15 minutes of meditation, and then 15-20 minutes on reflection. By spreading these out, I've found that it's easy to fit into my day, and I promise — if I can do it, you can too.

This routine helps me stay grounded. I've found that on days when I skip it, I'm quicker to get stressed or frustrated. But when I stick to it, everything feels smoother. It's like brushing your teeth — a small investment in keeping your mental "hygiene" in good shape. If I've learned anything from my own journey, it's that change takes time, and that's okay. Practicing gratitude and mindfulness isn't about aiming for perfection or becoming a flawless version of yourself. It's about making peace with who you are, learning to face life's ups and downs with a little more patience, and giving yourself permission to enjoy the good moments as they come.

Start small. Write down a few things you're grateful for each day. Take a couple of mindful moments when you can. Over time, these small steps add up, and you'll start to feel the shift. Life will still throw challenges, but with mindfulness and gratitude, you'll be able to face them with a little more strength and maybe even a sense of humor.

One more thing: life gets busy, and I'm not perfect at sticking to this all the time. But for me, that's okay. My goal isn't to check off boxes but to build habits that help me grow.

Beyond the practices I mentioned, there are basic things I need to keep in check. If you've been through some tough stuff (and most of us have), you may know how easy it is to let certain habits slide. For me, things like staying hydrated, eating well, and getting regular sleep plays a big part in my mental health. When I start slacking on those basics, I notice a big difference in my mindset.

Staying balanced isn't about being perfect. It's about noticing when something's off and making small adjustments. If I realize I've been eating junk for a few days, I'll make an effort to bring more balance back into my meals. If my sleep's been chaotic, I'll make a point to rest when I can during the day. And caffeine — let's just say I had to learn to be careful. It's hard to be patient and calm when you're buzzing on too much coffee, so I try to cut myself off by a certain time so I can actually sleep.

You might be wondering, "Is there any science behind this, or is it all just feel-good advice?" Well, good news: there's solid research that backs up how mindfulness helps us in practical, everyday ways. Practicing mindfulness can change the way our brain responds to stress and emotions. It's like mental weightlifting — the more we practice it, the stronger and more resilient our brains become.

Mindfulness is simple, really. It's about being in the moment, observing what's happening without judgment. And there are tons of ways to practice it. Here are a few tools that work for me:

- Journaling: Writing things down is one of the best ways to clear out all the thoughts bouncing around in your head. Sometimes, I journal about specific topics, like gratitude, and other times, I just write whatever comes up. If you're not into writing, try recording voice memos on your phone. Hearing your own thoughts can give you a clearer sense of what's going on around you.

- Meditation: Don't get hung up on the idea of meditation. You just have to take a moment to be still and breathe. You can meditate anywhere — while working out, painting, driving, or even just sitting quietly. Meditation is basically mindfulness in action, and it's one of the best tools I've found for staying calm.

- Grounding Techniques: When I'm feeling stressed, I use grounding techniques to bring myself back to the present. One of my go-to's is the 5-4-3-2-1 exercise: notice five things you can see, four you can touch, three you can hear, two you can smell, and one you can taste. It sounds simple, but it works. If it doesn't feel right, try one of the many breathing exercises; the point of grounding is to bring you back to the right now.

- Mantras: I keep a few mantras handy for when I feel overwhelmed. My favorite is, "What if it works out?" I'll repeat it to remind myself that not every situation has to be negative. Sometimes, I use the serenity prayer as well. Mantras can be anything that gives you a second to breathe and see the situation from a different angle.

If mindfulness is about seeing things as they are, gratitude is about celebrating the good that's there, even if it's small. This practice is a huge help, especially if you've been through tough times or have a tendency to focus on the negative. Gratitude is like training your brain to see the positives that we often overlook.

I started with just three things each morning, and over time, I noticed that my brain was naturally scanning for good moments throughout the day. Gratitude rewires the brain in a way that can be incredibly powerful for shifting our perspective. And it's not about pretending everything's perfect; it's about learning to notice the small, everyday things that bring a little light into your life.

I can't stress enough how important physical health is to mental well-being. It's not a magic cure, but staying hydrated, eating balanced meals, and getting enough sleep make a huge difference. When my body's not well-rested or nourished, my mind feels off. And if you're in a tough spot, basic self-care is often one of the first things we let slide. But you're worth taking care of. If we ignore our basic needs, it adds more stress to our minds, making it harder to move forward.

So, take a few minutes to assess how you can care for yourself physically. It might seem simple, but sometimes, these small adjustments have the biggest impact. And remember, this isn't about being perfect. It's about making choices that support your mental and physical health, one small step at a time.

When I started learning about mindfulness and gratitude, a lot of what I read made it sound almost mystical like there was some special trick to it. It felt hard to relate to at first. But as I practiced it more, I realized it's just about learning to focus on what's right in front of you. Don't worry about getting it perfect or fitting some specific mold. Your journey with mindfulness and gratitude will be your own, and it's okay if it looks different from someone else's.

If meditating in the morning doesn't work for you, try practicing it while doing something else, like going for a walk or cooking. And don't get caught up in the details or fancy techniques. This is your journey, and the real reward is in how it helps you grow, bit by bit.

Spirit Of Mindfulness And Gratitude

When I'm in need of a little extra motivation or perspective, I often turn to quotes that resonate with the mindset I'm working to build. I find quotes to be motivational, and if I'm having a tough day or need to regroup my thoughts, reflecting on a few good quotes helps. Here are a few favorites that capture the spirit of mindfulness and gratitude:

"As we express our gratitude, we must never forget that the highest appreciation is not to utter words, but to live by them."

—John F. Kennedy

"I am happy because I'm grateful. I choose to be grateful. That gratitude allows me to be happy."

—Will Arnett

"Mindfulness gives you time. Time gives you choices. Choices, skillfully made, lead to freedom."

—Bhante H. Gunaratana

"You can't stop the waves, but you can learn to surf."

—Jon Kabat-Zinn

"These mountains that you are carrying, you were only supposed to climb."

—Najwa Zebian

Each of these quotes holds a reminder that growth, peace, and happiness aren't about changing everything overnight. They're about the small, daily choices we make to be present, to appreciate what's good, and to keep moving forward, one step at a time.

In the end, practicing gratitude and mindfulness isn't about becoming perfect or even totally calm. It's about learning to handle life's ups and downs with a little more grace and a lot less stress. You don't have to do it all at once. Start small, stay consistent, and let yourself feel the shift as it happens.

And remember, you're not alone on this path. Every day is a new chance to try again, to be kind to yourself, and to enjoy the journey, bumps and all.

Joshua Barrett

___

Chapter Ten:
Continual Growth And Learning

"Anyone who has never made a mistake has never tried anything new."

—Albert Einstein

If you are going to try new things, if you are going to push yourself out of your comfort zone, you are going to make mistakes. And that's okay. In fact, that's where the real learning happens. If we are always holding tight to what we already know, too afraid to mess up, we are not really growing—we are just standing still.

Don't Be A Know It All

One of the most important lessons I have learned is that growth starts with being open. And sometimes, being open means setting aside what you think you already know. For years, I thought being confident meant knowing all the answers, or at least pretending to. But that attitude doesn't just hold you back; it shuts down new possibilities before they even have a chance to grow. I was building walls with my own pride, and all they did was keep me stuck.

Then I came across this quote from Socrates: "All I know is that I know nothing." It seemed so counterintuitive at first, but I finally understood it. Real confidence doesn't come from knowing everything. It comes from knowing that you still have so much to learn—and that you are okay with that. By admitting that I don't have it all figured out, I am giving myself permission to grow, learn, and change. It sounds simple, but it's been one of the biggest shifts in my life.

Letting go of what we think we know can be one of the best ways to open ourselves up to new perspectives. For example, we often believe we know how others should act based on how we'd handle the same situation. But the truth is everyone's experience is different. When we project our perspective onto others, we are not really seeing them—we are just reinforcing our own assumptions. By approaching situations with openness, by saying, "I don't know everything," we are more likely to actually learn something new and, more importantly, to truly understand the people around us.

Develop Empathy And Let Go Of Assumptions

Empathy Begins When We Let Go of Expectations. How often do we expect people to act or think like we do? We might not even realize it, but we tend to filter other people's actions through our own experiences. It's like trying to fit everyone into a mold that's shaped for us. When they don't fit, things feel off because we are not seeing them as they truly are; we are seeing them through the constraints of our own assumptions.

But when you start to let go of these assumptions, something amazing happens. You start seeing things as they are. Instead of judging others for not acting the way you would, you begin to understand where they are coming from. You step out of your own shoes and try on someone else's for a change. This has been huge for me in building empathy. It's helped me see that everyone's journey is unique and that understanding someone else often starts with letting go of your own perspective.

This shift is especially powerful when it comes to healing. When you are dealing with pain or trauma, it's easy to fall into black-and-white thinking. We tell ourselves that things are either "this way" or "that way," and there's no middle ground. But that kind of thinking can keep us trapped in our own pain. It's like building a prison out of certainty.

Mistakes Are Opportunities For Growth

Real healing comes when we open ourselves up to shades of gray, to new ideas and ways of coping. Your mind is like a device that needs regular updates. You wouldn't keep using an old version of your phone's software without updates. The same goes for your mind. If you let yourself "update" by letting in new perspectives, you are setting yourself up for growth. The process isn't easy, but it's necessary.

One of the biggest myths about self-improvement is that it happens quickly. But real growth doesn't work that way. Change is gradual, and it requires consistency. When I first started practicing meditation each morning, I'd do it grudgingly, checking off a box. But over time, that routine became something I looked forward to. It went from being a task to becoming a vital part of my day. Now, it's something I wouldn't want to skip.

If you are just starting out, remember that it takes time. You won't feel transformed overnight. But if you keep showing up, day after day, those small changes add up. This is like planting a tree. You don't dig it up every day to see if it's growing. You water it, give it sunlight, and let it take its own time. Growth is the same way—quiet, slow, and often invisible. But it's happening.

During those long stretches where it feels like nothing is changing, don't lose heart. Every day that you show up and put in the work, you are making progress, even if you can't see it right away. Change builds up gradually, like water carving a path through stone. It's a process, and as long as you are moving forward, you are growing. The important thing is to stay consistent, even when it feels slow.

Find Strength In Community And Forgiveness

An essential lesson for me is that you are not meant to do life alone. We need people around us, a support system that keeps us grounded. For years, I tried to go it alone, thinking I didn't need anyone. But thinking that way only kept me stuck. When I started opening up to others and allowed myself to be part of a community, I realized how much strength I could draw from it.

So many people have helped me on my journey, and being open to new ideas and experiences allowed these interactions to have life-changing effects.

Early in my recovery, a guy approached me at a meeting and said, "I'm going to sponsor you. Meet me here on Sunday." I didn't really want a sponsor, but I went anyway. And week after week, he showed up for me. He listened, he didn't judge, and he taught me how to process my pain. He gave me tools for living a life I could actually be proud of. Now, I sponsor others because I know how much a helping hand can mean. Had I not been open to what he had to say, I would have missed out on the life I have today.

When I hit rock bottom, I ended up on probation for a year. I was pretty freaked out to go and expected it to be a very unpleasant experience; at the end of my first meeting, my Probation officer said," I can tell you have experienced a lot of pain, and you just need some love so for the next year, you will at least get that." That meeting changed my life forever; I had just started my recovery journey and only had a little bit of sober time. I was struggling with my self-worth and was overwhelmed by the mess I had made of my life. Her patience and compassion started a drive in me. After I had a few years of sobriety, I remember reflecting on everything Officer Anderson did for me by simple caring. Her kindness was one of the driving forces behind my compassion today. It is amazing what we can learn from each other when we are open and honest about how little we know. There are hundreds of interactions and people I could recall that changed my life and influenced the person I am today. The important part is allowing yourself to be open.

Your support system could be friends, family, a recovery group, or even a therapist. The important thing is that you let people in. Yes, healing is personal work, but it's enhanced by the connections we have with others. Community isn't just a nice addition to life; it's a necessity. The people around you help make the burden of life bearable, especially on days when you feel you can't carry it alone. They are like backup power when you are running on empty.

Forgiveness is another essential part of growth, and it doesn't always come easy. Sometimes, you have to wait for others to catch up to the changes you are making in yourself. I remember reaching out to my father-in-law to make amends. I thought he'd immediately see the progress I'd made and be ready to forgive. But he wasn't. He wasn't even ready to talk. That was tough to accept.

Over time, I tried again and again until, one day, he was finally willing to meet me halfway. I learned that forgiveness isn't always a one-time thing. It's a process that takes patience, both with yourself and with others. Just because you are ready to move forward doesn't mean everyone else is on the same timeline. That experience taught me the importance of respecting each person's journey. You can only control your own actions, so focus on keeping your side of the street clean and let others come around in their own time.

We live in a world that likes things to be black and white. But the reality is life is full of gray areas. One of the biggest challenges I had to overcome was letting go of my own judgments and being open to perspectives I didn't agree with. Sometimes, we think people need to have the same opinions, beliefs, or backgrounds as we do to be worth listening to. But that's just not true.

One of the best things you can do for yourself is to break down those walls and allow yourself to learn from everyone around you, not just those who think like you. Sometimes, the most valuable insights come from people you'd never expect. Being open to different perspectives is like stretching your mind; it helps you see the world in more detail. The truth often lies in the gray areas, and the more open you are to seeing it, the more you'll grow.

Consistency Is A Key

Routine is the backbone of growth. This journey requires you to show up, even on the days you don't want to. When I started on this path, I would get frustrated during the times when change seemed painfully slow or when others couldn't see the progress I was making. But I realized that the daily effort was what mattered most. It's like training a muscle: you have to keep working it, even when you don't see results right away.

Remember, setbacks are part of the process. Some days will be harder than others, and sometimes, it'll feel like you're moving backward. But each little victory counts. Celebrate them, use them as fuel, and keep going. When you commit to your routine, you are building a foundation for lasting change. The results may not show up immediately, but with consistency, you'll start to notice shifts in how you think, feel and respond to life.

The journey of growth and learning never really ends. Even now, I keep my routines and stay committed to my practices, not because I think I'll reach some "final version" of myself, but because it's a part of who I am. I've come to love the process, even the tough parts, because each day brings something new.

Your life matters. Who you are, what you have been through—all of it matters. If you are reading this, I want you to know that you are needed here, with all your quirks and uniqueness. Life is tough, but you are tougher. And as long as you keep moving, you are growing. Remember, you don't have to do it alone. There are people out there who care, who understand, and who want to help you on your journey.

Keep going, keep learning, and keep being open to everything life has to teach you. This isn't the end of the road; it's just the beginning. And trust me, you have got this.

Go Be Love!

www.ingramcontent.com/pod-product-compliance
Lightning Source LLC
Chambersburg PA
CBHW061700120626
46550CB00003B/1017